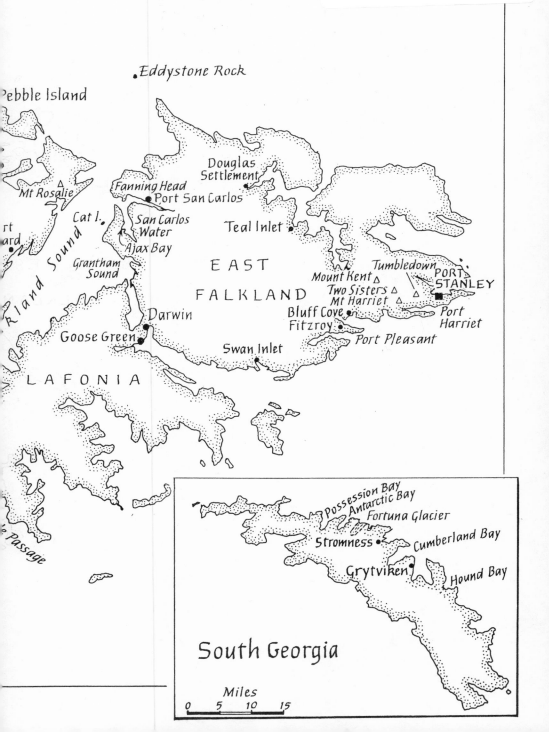

. Eddystone Rock

Pebble Island

Mt Rosalie △

Fanning Head
● Port San Carlos

Douglas
Settlement
.

San Carlos
Water

Cat I.
.

Ajax Bay

Teal Inlet .

EAST

FALKLAND

Grantham
Sound

Tumbledown
Mount Kent △
Two Sisters △
Mt Harriet △
Bluff Cove .
Fitzroy .

PORT
STANLEY
■

Port
Harriet

Port Pleasant

Darwin

Goose Green

LAFONIA

Swan Inlet

Falkland Sound

Passage

Possession Bay
Antarctic Bay
Fortuna Glacier

Stromness .

Cumberland Bay

Grytviken .

Hound Bay

South Georgia

Miles

0   5   10   15

HER MAJESTY'S INTERROGATOR

By the same author:

Her Majesty's Vietnam Soldier

HER MAJESTY'S INTERROGATOR

by

GUY BRANSBY

LEO COOPER
LONDON

First published in Great Britain in 1996 by
LEO COOPER
190 Shaftesbury Avenue, London WC2H 8JL
an imprint of
Pen & Sword Books Ltd,
47 Church Street,
Barnsley, South Yorkshire S70 2AS

A CIP record for this book is available from the British Library

ISBN 0 85052 471 7

Typeset by CentraCet Limited, Cambridge
in 11/13 Garamond

Printed in Great Britain by Redwood Books, Trowbridge, Wilts

TO
GUY FRANCISCO
AND
CARMEN PILAR

CONTENTS

A Pathan Chief ponders British battlefield dead on the North West Indian Frontier in the Nineteenth Century:

'These were not stirred by anger,
   Nor yet by lust made bold;
Renown they thought above them,
   Nor did they look for gold.
To them their leader's signal
   Was as the voice of God:
Unmoved and uncomplaining,
   The path it showed they trod.

As, without sound or struggle,
   The stars unhurrying march,
Where Allah's finger guides them,
   Through yonder purple arch,
These Franks, sublimely silent,
   Without a quickened breath,
Went, in the strength of duty,
   Straight to their goal of death.'

(From a Pushtu ballad; recounted in English by Sir Francis Hastings Doyle as 'The Red Thread of Honour'.)

ACKNOWLEDGEMENT

I am grateful to the Commandant General of the Royal Air Force Regiment, Air Commodore T.G. Thorn AFC FRAeS RAF, and his Staff, for permission to quote the motto of the Corps' No 3 Wing and for notes on its history.

FOREWORD

The story that follows is true. However, as with the account of my passage through the Indo-China wars in the sixties (*Her Majesty's Vietnam Soldier*) and with the next tale, of service with a United Nations' military force in the India/Pakistan war and in Northern Ireland (*Her Majesty's Peacekeeper*), I have not identified my companions, friend or foe, too precisely.

The times of which I write are not long ago and, as a lower-level participant, who can only write of detailed, localized 'scenes', I must not set anyone, who doubtless did what seemed like a good idea at the time, up for critical scrutiny today.

This story involves the shadowy, and previously unrecounted, world of the military Interrogator, but, for obvious reasons, the detail of British methods of military interrogation may not be revealed.

As with my previous chronicles, I have tried to let the self-indulgent and slow-thinking, but I hope well-intentioned, younger man that I was then talk to you as he would have done, without improving his aspect by possible later wisdom.

A steely-eyed, firm-jawed, unflinchingly courageous traditional British schoolboy-type hero, who fortunately exists in reasonable numbers, should have gone to my five conflicts in my place; perhaps he could have told inspiring tales. However, maybe my accounts can be a sort of tribute to the probable majority of more or less unsuitable 'warrior champions' who, to their dismay, suddenly find themselves on the centre stage of violent and dramatic events of contemporary history – and attempt to cope.

GB

PROLOGUE

Driving the two Argentine prisoners-of-war from Goose Green ahead of us at a forced pace over the slippery mud patches and the tripping tussock clumps, my fellow Interrogator and I gradually closed in on the British land forces field command post at San Carlos.

There were murmurings of 'Nazis' and some barely audible hisses and boos. These observations were not directed at the enemy, but at the Sergeant and myself. The Marines and Paratroopers, who covered the hillsides that extended back from the shore, felt sympathy for fellow infantrymen at the mercy of a sinister and underhanded force.

Our troops knew who we were because, as we were the only ex-South Georgia recapture men on the Falklands, we had initially been the only members of this Task Force to have met the Argentine military. We had briefed units on our impressions and had made a few points on POW handling.

We believed that we had important information as to exactly which enemy units were at the Goose Green battle. Thus they could be crossed off the already known overall Argentine orbat and our General could have a reasonable idea of how much more he had to face.

Our prisoners, a Lieutenant and a Sergeant, were going to confirm our information and answer any further queries, if our luck and persuasiveness held, from the senior officers in the command post.

They were not bad chaps, quite dignified under their ordeal. The shock of battle, the uncertainty of what capture might bring and the regular discomfort of outdoor life in the Falklands had caused them, and others, to be quite malleable. Under other circumstances they were types one would have enjoyed having a beer with, or, in their case, perhaps a glass of wine or pisco.

A Marine had driven us across San Carlos Water from Ajax Bay in his 'rigid-raider' and had put us ashore at the Settlement jetty. I did this journey many times a day. Local field command was at San Carlos

I

and my POW centre was at Ajax Bay. I would be told at the former location what information was wanted and I would return to the latter and, with the help of my two SNCOs, try to get it.

Waves of movement coursed through the troops we passed as heads turned towards the various unit trenches where the Signallers sat on permanent 'listening-watch'.

'Air-raid Red!' was murmured through the ranks and everyone unconcernedly carried on with whatever they were doing. We had ceased to react too agitatedly to this warning as it meant that some part of the widely spread Task Force was being bombed. However, we did, of course, cast our eyes around the cold, clear sky. As always on clear days, which had come to be known as 'air-raid days', there was a strong wind blowing. It would have been a good day for drying clothes on a line.

The only thing that would have perturbed us, at this stage of the campaign, would have been if someone had shouted out the in-theatre innovation of 'Air-raid Immediate'.

'Air-raid Immediate!' roared a Signaller at the top of his voice.

Before the majority could even dive into their trenches, the scream of jetfighters irrupted into our world.

'*Ataque aéreo!*' I shouted at the bewildered Argentines.

'*Sus aviones!*' my Sergeant said with mock anger to the Argentine Sergeant as he grabbed the POW's arm and began pulling his counterpart across the tussock faster than he could really run.

I followed, with their Officer jogging at my side. I thought that he looked almost embarrassed and apologetic.

My 'Unit' of three Interrogators had dug ourselves a trench at San Carlos for just such a contingency. It could accommodate more than the standard British infantry trench because we were invariably accompanied by prisoners. The Geneva Convention leaves no doubt; once they are captured and disarmed, they must be treated like your own. Our trench was the lowest one on the long slope that went down to the sea. The beach and the water were only a few metres in front of us.

There were several explosions and an eruption of smoke from Ajax Bay. Some of our companions were being killed or maimed by this arbitrary and impersonal method of warfare. I became aware of the commotion on the sea to our front. There was a furious undulating chatter from the parked ships as their deck-mounted machine guns poured tracer bullets into the sky.

A Mirage raced magnificently across our front and two great pillars of sea water straddled a British warship.

The Marines and the Paras had been present at the much bigger air-raids that had taken place a few days earlier. I had been on board a Royal Navy vessel, able to have a meal and a drink in the Wardroom, at the time. I had mixed feelings about having missed these events!

As one's little inflatable boat skimmed San Carlos Water, it travelled over the dark corpse of a British warship that could be seen through the icy water fathoms below. She was still dying and shed the very last of her life in great bubbles of compressed air. Oil and the belongings that she had once held for her sailors streamed from her.

There seemed to be only four enemy aircraft in the vicinity and they appeared to be exclusively on a run that included the nearer ships and Ajax Bay. It looked as if there was no danger to us at San Carlos. We started to stand up in our trenches and then to climb up on to the front parapets for a better view. The scene may have been a terrible one but there cannot be a more riveting spectator sport.

There were bangs and whooshes as missiles streaked away from the warships. An aircraft, totally without warning, exploded in a fireball of instantly igniting aviation fuel to our front. The men around spontaneously cried out in awe and horror. Pieces appeared to fly off a more distant aircraft and it began a graceful downward curve. Then it too suddenly erupted in a bright orange flash and scattered itself across the sea. A dart of giddying nausea shot through me at the thought of a man burning alive, prior to his disintegration.

The attacking aircraft seemed to have vanished. The fire from the ships tailed off and we had just started exclaiming to each other about the sights we had seen when a shattering roar erupted from the earth around us as a Mirage rose above the crest of a hill behind and tore down the slope on to us. Its downdraught parted the tussock beneath its belly and its wings seemed low enough to saw a man in half. We hurled ourselves into our trenches and the sky was blotted out for a second.

It must have been my pre-Vietnam training from over thirteen years earlier – practising the lightning snap-shot on those jungle ranges – for I cocked my sub-machine carbine with a blow from my left palm while flicking the safety-catch to 'automatic' with my right thumb. Ahead of everyone, I popped up on the front of my trench and poured my entire 30-round magazine after the vanishing aircraft.

The Sterling sub-machine gun is a small 9mm, mostly self-defence, weapon. The Mirage was probably flying faster than its muzzle velocity. My bullets, when they had run out of power, would have just rattled onto the shingly beach a little way in front of me.

Men were emerging from the ground and staring at me in amazement. The Argentines checked themselves in case I had shot them and their Sergeant crossed himself.

As a British Officer who had occasionally done original things for nearly twenty years, I had developed a few aids for preventing people, particularly superiors, from worrying for too long. Play to the gallery, I decided.

'Take that,' I bellowed in a high-pitched exaggeratedly public school accent, waving my fist at the, by now, distant speck. 'Let that be a lesson to you; You Dago bounder!' I finished with an old-fashioned affronted English gentleman look.

Men fell back shrieking into their waterlogged holes.

PART I

Inadvertent, Appropriate
Pre-Falklands War Preparation

'PREPAREMUS BELLUM'*

(The motto of 3 Wing, Royal Air Force Regiment. Above the scroll containing these words on the Wing crest is the design of three winged Roman javelins. The Wing was formed at El Hamra in 1951 and, after active service in the near and middle East, moved to Royal Air Force Station Catterick in 1975. The station is on the site of a Roman military camp. The crest was, of course, prepared by the Royal College of Heralds and authorized by Her Majesty The Queen. However, the original inspiration for it was that of the Wing's first Catterick Commanding Officer, Wing Commander Marcus Witherow. He subsequently rose to the rank of Air Commodore. The Wing's men went into combat from the Unit's conception. They served in Cyprus and Aden, in the Oman War, Northern Ireland, the Falklands War, the Gulf War and with a number of United Nations' military actions. Sadly, the Wing was a victim of the 1993 defence cuts.

In 1980 the author was Wing Adjutant and served with one of its Sub-Units, 15 Squadron, in Northern Ireland.)

'Aha!' the Second-in-Command of the Royal Air Force Regiment Training Wing bellowed cheerily down the telephone to a Staff Officer at the Directorate in London at a few minutes after eight o'clock on the first military working day of 1982. There had been a week's break, for those not on essential duty, that had included Christmas and New Year's Day. He was getting a policy decision on an infantry training matter I had raised.

'You're back at last!' he roared on and gave a brief routine burst of honking laughter. He was very much a 'Yoiks, Tally-Ho' type.

* Let us prepare for war.

7

'Yes', he continued, winking at me. 'Just like us, trying to shake off the festive duff, sipping the year's first cup of Service tea.' He beamed at me and was obviously hardly able to contain himself. 'And bracing yourself for the war of 1982!'

I sincerely, but more restrainedly, joined his thunderous explosion of guffaws at the total absurdity of such an idea.

Despite my age and experience, I was a junior level training officer. I had only recently transferred back to mainland British forces from the New Zealand Army and to the soldier corps of the Royal Air Force. When I had moved from the Royal Artillery to the Royal New Zealand Artillery over ten years earlier my military clock of life had also been wound back to the beginning.

As a transferee cannot have passed all the various in-house hurdles-to-progress of his new establishment, his well-documented, almost identical past progression is rarely counted, and suddenly-arriving outsider war veterans become marked men to some unmedalled superiors. Repeating apprenticeships of many years is also, of course, discouraging and performance is unlikely to be as dynamic as on the first excited youthful one. This appears to justify the treatment.

However, I was happy with my lot. I had for the past five years had a classically lovely young Latin-American wife and, subsequently, a small sturdy son and a tiny, pretty and cheeky baby daughter. The three of them filled my every moment and thought with joy.

I rented a fine house in a picturesque North Yorkshire village, adjacent to the base I operated from. I had good colleagues, good neighbours and good friends. I loved the physical fresh-air life of a military training officer, the company of my skilled and enthusiastic NCO assistants and the company of the keen young troops. Few can have been more blessed than I.

Even if I had known that my domestic happiness had not much time left to run, I doubt if I should have believed it. When I count up its pathetically few years, I am always surprised at how short the era of family life in my own country was – it so fills my memory.

It had been a wrench to the heart to leave the New Zealanders. After three years as an Officer in the British Army, I had volunteered to serve with the ANZAC in the Vietnam war. I had two tours of duty to two very different parts of the jungle war; and a two-year posting to a mountain war with the UN in Kashmir had followed. I also had several brief training visits to the Royal Fiji Military Forces. In 1980 family reasons had prompted a return to mainland British forces. The RAF Regiment was one of the few 'growth industries' in the British military at the time and honoured me with a job offer.

The RAF Regiment can trace its ancestry to 1915 and the Royal Flying Corps' Rolls Royce armoured car companies in the Middle East. These Units, later part of the RAF, fought on after the First World War, during the 1920s and 1930s, in support of established Arab régimes against insurgent movements. During World War Two, in February, 1942, various ground parts of the RAF (eg Ground Gunners), and transferring Army infantrymen, were formed into the Corps of the RAF Regiment with its army style of dress and distinctive shoulder flashes ('mudguards'). The new Corps had mostly ex-Royal Marines and ex-Brigade of Guards NCOs and Warrant Officers and ex-British Indian Army Officers. It went into action almost from the moment of its founding and some elements of the Corps have been fighting, usually for the wider protection of RAF assets, somewhere in the world to this day.

Sir Winston Churchill was an enthusiastic sponsor of the new force and wanted it to be a truly independent Corps like the Royal Marines. However, it appears that the fighter pilots, who cannot seem to cope with any threat to their rule of the RAF, renegued and made the RAF Regiment just a part of one of their ground 'Branches'.

The corps was over 80,000 strong by the end of the Second World War and had a paratroop element, besides infantry, light armour, anti-aircraft guns and missiles, a ceremonial unit and training establishments. It was particularly savaged by the defence cuts of the 1990s and now numbers only a few thousand. A senior fighter pilot is usually appointed Commandant General. In the 1950s the RAF made the corps wear blue uniforms for a while on active service.

The RAF Regiment and its ancestors also raised, and commanded, native levy forces for the Empire: the Iraq Levies in 1915, the Aden Protectorate Levies in the 1930s and the RAF Regiment Malaya, in the 1940s. These courageous, disciplined and smart army-style colonial soldiers gave constant sterling service (the companies of Kurds were particularly magnificent) until British influence was withdrawn from their regions during the 1960s.

The RAF Regiment has done more fighting than any other part of the RAF since 1945 and, in company with the fighter pilots, is one of the only two 'teeth arms' (ie a force that is armed, trained and designated for offensive action) of the RAF.

Though I am not altogether suited to be a soldier, I enlisted in the British Army because the older members of my peer group were among the last conscripts and I felt honour bound, or something like that, to join them. I transferred to the New Zealand Army because my time with the British was, apart from Iron Curtain patrols, largely spent either on a training area or poodlefaking. I felt that this time would be wasted if I did not put to some use the experience that, with my natural disadvantages, had been very hard-earned. Helping to hold up communist imperialism in South East Asia had not seemed a bad crusade. After doing the world this favour, I expected to sink back to poodlefaking, and perhaps a few better things, in the civilian world. However, every time I started to get this organized, an order to attend another warlike campaign would crop up. I have no general regrets. *Insh-Allah*.

At the time of my transfer to it, the RAF Regiment was expanding into interesting and challenging areas of new pattern light armour and ever more modern anti-aircraft missiles. Within three weeks of joining my new Corps I was hit in the ribs by a most professionally guided Irish Republican brick, near the Falls Park, while attached to a Royal Fusiliers' patrol.

In Indo-China I was in my twenties; I served in Kashmir and Ireland in my thirties; as I stood before the training Second-in-Command's desk on that early January, 1982, day I was a few weeks short of my fortieth birthday.

Most basic things had not changed since my own first training nearly twenty years earlier. They had not changed because men and terrain do not change. Fighting men must be battlefield fit and they must know how to move on, live on, and attack or defend a variety of locations and objects. If policies on such matters have evolved from a heritage of combat experience, it is unlikely, unless there is a revolutionary change of weaponry, that they can be fundamentally improved, and certainly not by peacetime theory. Weaponry seems to change slightly about every half-generation, but usually not so traumatically that even the oldest soldiers cannot adapt during their service.

The standard British infantry weapon was still the Self-Loading Rifle (SLR) as it had been in my youth. It is a Royal Ordnance Factory adaption of the Belgian Fabrique Nationale (FN) fully automatic rifle. The British had made it single shot to encourage our musketry principle that 'every shot must be an aimed shot' and to prevent soldiers from wasting ammunition. The SLR of the 1960s had a brown polished wood stock and the 1980s version had one of black plastic.

Unfortunately the rank and file of all possible, and actual, enemies of Britain of the day had Eastern European or Chinese fully automatic weapons. Thus assaulting British troops closed in on men who were all armed with machine guns. The Argentines had the fully automatic pukka Belgian FN, both the latest version, including some with a neat fold-away butt to aid a Tommy-gun stance, and some originals.

I heard, after the war, that some Argentine soldiers lamented the age of their weapons. However, if offered a choice between the newest British SLR and an FN made in the 1950s, I should bear in mind that there was far more craftsmanship in manufacture in earlier times and, after all, so long as it has been well looked after, a fully-automatic weapon is a fully-automatic weapon.

During the fairly short periods that I had actually been in New Zealand, during the time I had worn a New Zealand uniform, training had become my specialization and I had risen to the command of training companies. However, I was privileged to have been able to get back home with a job when I needed to, privileged to still be in Her Majesty's Service and, in spite of it being not well-known and totally unsung, I was privileged to be in one of the most dedicated and professional soldierly organizations, at its junior levels, that I have ever been associated with.

It did not bother me, therefore, when men much younger than myself, and without active service, but who held the positions that I once had, exercised what was their right and duty by pulling up alongside my training position in their Landrover and 'sorting us all out'. I was theoretically back about fifteen years, running small-arms ranges, concerning myself with the minutiae thereof and doubling in with assaults as if I were a fresh-faced youth again.

Bad eggs were practically non-existent among my trainees. They too brought me happiness and delight. To an extent I could live again, through them, the sense of achievement, without quite so much of the anxiety, of my own basic soldier training days at Mons Officer Cadet School in the mid-1960s. I could see again the faces and characters of my young friends, now scattered.

*

The first months of 1982 jogged idyllically along, despite, or perhaps because of, the cold, damp and snow of North Yorkshire. The weather gave a greater challenge to life and a greater satisfaction in training achievement. It made the cosy open-fired warmth of loving homes even more wonderful.

Apart from Latin eyes that would one day devastate generations of maidens as then unborn, my son has a solid Anglo-Saxon frame. When only four years old, he loved to walk ten or fifteen miles with me through the vales and dales beside the banks of the River Swale. On hillside tracks and along tree-lined footpaths he would talk to me importantly of his life at home, of camp and village friends, of his tiny pre-school and would recount his philosophies. He was at the age of rather difficult questions ('What happens when you die, Daddy?'). We would examine ancient ruins en route, pause excitedly at glimpses of interesting wild life and often stay at country inns, in Reeth and other places, overnight.

I would have his little blazer, grey trousers, shirt, shoes and tie in my pack with my own smarter clothes for the restaurant in the evening. We loved making an occasion of events when we could. It made everything even more special.

My tiny daughter had started to walk the summer before the South Atlantic war, or rather, she had started to run. She was only ten months old and her only method of not falling flat on her face was to keep up a cracking momentum. She found even greater stability if she used her push-chair like a sort of wheeled Zimmer-frame.

She was clever at escaping from me if I was momentarily distracted. However, she was not difficult to find. One scanned the area for a push-chair that raced randomly, and apparently unaidedly, about in every direction.

Her first day of self-propulsion was the day of our village fair. Despite my efforts, she regularly slipped away and I was horrified to see whole lines of good citizens suddenly drop in various areas of the crowded green as the backs of their knees were struck from under them. However, these were the strong and kindly people of North Yorkshire. They waved away my frantic apologies and beamed at the dark baby girl, her big eyes looking around crossly at those who had been inadvertently standing with their backs towards her on routes that she had not known that she wished to travel along.

My wife had not been permitted by her Colonel father to take up an offer to be a cover girl for Spanish-language fashion magazines because she had still been a schoolgirl at the time. I had married her shortly after that. She was long-legged, willowy and instinctively graceful and elegant. Her glinting dark hair and eyes, her pale olive skin, lovely mouth and glittering, even white smile hypnotised. Men envied me.

It is certain that I did not pause as often as I should have to pinch myself and wonder how a former 'Champagne Charlie' and ever marginal competent could have been selected for first prize category personal circumstances. There were noisy, beery and hilarious, but inoffensive, end-of-course celebrations when my NCO instructors, graduating trainees and I would drink and dine together. We would finally bid them farewell from the Depot and send them forth to soldierhood after a ceremonial parade before our unrelievedly dedicated, immaculate and inflexibly honourable Commandant. The RAF Regiment Band would play the tunes of glory for them, including 'Holyrood', the Corps march, as their families looked on proudly.

I remember being rather disappointed that, by the 1980s, bayonet fighting was one of the few things that had been dropped from the Basic Training syllabus. Some high-ranking theorist had no doubt decided that we were all far too technological by then for such primitive behaviour. I was not disappointed because I was wiser, but because it was good fun, and one always had the total interest and participation of the troops; all that screaming, charging and dis-embowelling of sandbags. So I used to give each of my courses an informal talk on some occasion while we waited for trucks to turn up or were having a tea break. Gripping a borrowed trainee's rifle with a fixed bayonet, or my shooting-stick, in the 'on guard' stance and absolutely wallowing in the chance to overact to the ultimate degree, I would hurl myself at an imaginary foe. I would do the unnerving blood-curdling scream, the face hideously contorted into a demon of hate, and with unblinking Tiger-eyes would charge bombastically forward.

I would pause for a moment or two at this point to explain the important principle of removing any risk to oneself from the enemy soldier's bayonet before attempting to run him through. One must dash his weapon to one side and, while he was off balance, swing your own rifle butt round to smash him in the head and send him to the ground. On this firm base one could skewer him, ideally through the upper stomach, up under the rib cage and through the diaphragm, or in the throat. I would finally, again with maximum histrionics, go through the motions of what I had just explained. If there was time before the next activity, as this was an unofficial extra, I would spread the troops out and exhort them to imagine their way through the sequence as if a Hollywood movie mogul was observing them with his cheque book poised.

I was more than thankful that I had never been involved in any real bayonet fighting, neither could I think of the sort of conflict where it might ever crop up again, but a mention of it was good for impressing the trainees and broadening their general knowledge and vision of weaponry.

Bayonet fighting, of course, returned to the training programme after the Falklands war. In those old-fashioned Crimea-style battles that took place around Port Stanley, men died in accordance with the ten thousand years old tradition since the mining of metal was first learned; screaming in agony, terror and despair, they had a honed and sharpened blade shoved crudely and messily through their life-supporting organs by a fellow human being.

I had heard of the Falkland Islands before I went to the war. I even knew where South Georgia was.

On the wall of the courtyard outside the headmaster's office of the boarding school I attended, there was a politically out of date but high quality framed chart of the world (Africa and Asia were almost entirely pink). I would study it while waiting for my turn to give the vain old bully yet another go at his favourite goal of reducing totally captive small boys, who had been brought up to revere authority, to total misery. Minor boisterousness, unpunctuality and nonconformity would be misrepresented as irrefutable proof of a total lack of moral standards and nought but a wasted and hopeless life lay ahead.

My visits to the office were, of course, fairly regular and so I became agreeably familiar with the chart. Early on, I spotted the tiny, narrow, curved pink island because it was so alone in an Antarctic sea. Its loneliness made me shiver even on a sunny Surrey day. Other land and island groupings looked positively cosy by comparison; you just could not miss it. It became a sort of sad and remotely exiled friend and I would eagerly seek it out as soon as possible after the headmaster's ferret-faced male secretary had marched into the mid-morning class and announced to an instantly equally official-faced tutor that I was summoned. I could never have dreamed that I should one day stand on South Georgia and, fractionally, help to keep it pink.

I had read magazine articles on the Falkland Islands. I gathered that Captain James Cook and a few others, some of them foreign, had been to Antarctica in past centuries and subsequently, via whaling and a ship refitting station, a sturdy band of overseas British sheep farmers had evolved. I think that I thought the Islands got their name because they were almost identical in aspect to a Scots outer island. I did not realize that they had been named after a British Admiral. I had definitely never heard the words 'las Malvinas' or 'les Malouines'.

I even met a Falkland Islander about ten years before I went there. He was a young pilot in the Royal New Zealand Air Force and told me a bit about the place as we sat in an Auckland air base. I forgot much of what he said. At the time there had been no particular need to concentrate very hard.

Later, however, I was to encounter some far more detailed information on the Falklands and it impressed me. In Northern Ireland in late 1980 I came off a shift in a command post and sank gratefully into a battered armchair in the all-ranks rest room just as a current affairs film was starting on the TV. It had me incensed: it was a film of such clear-cut heroes and villains. The heroes were the interviewed islanders who had lived on and worked their hard, but beloved, land for one hundred and fifty years. They spoke reasonably and rationally. Their ancestry and culture were pure old-fashioned British. They could not comprehend a totally unnecessary and arbitrary proposed gift of them and theirs, by their government's Foreign Office, to a murderous, totalitarian South American military and police dictatorship, a government and a people with whom they had not a thing in common.

The villains were, of course, the shifty-eyed and prevaricating British Foreign Office officials in London who obviously wished to do a 'desk-clearing job' on the Falklands to convenience themselves. They clearly had no comprehension of, nor interest in, feelings which the British islanders, who they were paid to serve, held as strongly and as unquestioningly as a belief in God. Management of the islands must, sadly, have been allocated to the lowliest group in the Ministry. I sat alone and affronted, as I seethed over cloistered and pampered mandarins who seemed to me to be devoid of principle, loyalty, honour, a sense of obvious injustice and even a bit of local knowledge.

The interviewed Argentine officials were neutrals, neither heroes nor villains, because they had nothing to say that could be taken seriously. The Falklands were theirs because they were the inheritors of the Spanish Empire of one hundred and sixty years earlier; under this rule California and Texas must be returned to Mexico. They were theirs because they are part of the same continental shelf; Britain is on the continental shelf of several European countries. The islands were near to them as they were only four hundred miles away; most countries are on large land masses and their common borders are an infinite fraction thick, yet they are totally independent of each other and may have utterly different characters and populations.

It was quite obvious that the Argentines would listen only to their fanciful version of history and geography and just wanted the islands to make them feel grand and imperialistic and fan mercurial, but precarious, Latin egos. The documentary also mentioned that ownership of the Falklands would give them a great step towards Antarctica and any riches that might be there.

After their defeat, I spoke to Argentines who did not know that it was going to be cold and wet and had thought that they would be welcomed as liberators by fellow Latin-Americans who had been held by Britain against their will.

An investigative TV documentary on the Argentine a few months earlier had discovered that political dissidents were dropped, still living, into the South Atlantic from aircraft. For successive Argentine governments it seems that a bit of rabble-rousing over the Falklands has always been a useful way of making the population turn their eyes away from misery and injustice at home.

Almost as near to the Falkland Islands is Chile's piece of Atlantic coastline. Thus, if for some perverse reason one wished to give the islands away to a foreign country who had nothing to do with them, then Chile could perhaps be an alternative choice. I discovered, later, that the Falkland Islanders like the Chileans immensely. Those who have not visited South America often wrongly assume that the national characters are all the same. The islanders look upon Punta Arenas as their nearest city, have long-standing trading relationships with it, take shopping trips and vacations there and some, as an alternative to Britain, send their children there for the higher education that is not available on the islands. Chilean cowboys have been hired when extra hands were needed for stock roundups. Some remained and became citizens.

Even before the invasion the islanders traditionally disliked the Argentinians for, besides their covetousness, tourists who visited, and officials encountered during transit through Buenos Aires, were invariably impolite to them.

There and then, in my seedy Nissen hut and on the standard teeming Northern Ireland winter night, I was compelled to strike a blow! I, therefore, composed a letter; a real fire-breathing Blimpish thing: 'evil Latin American military dictators . . . stalwart overseas British, happy, pioneering, farming folk . . . craven behaviour, giving in to every greedy and unreasonable Argentine demand, etc, etc.'

I copied it out by hand sufficient times to send one to each of the main national British newspapers. None of them published it and, apart from the odd angry, randomly occurring thought or a few strong words in an Officers' Mess bar, which did not evoke excessive response, the daily problems of Northern Ireland gradually distracted my concern.

We should have been allowed to take the weak officials from the Falklands section of the Foreign Office with us to the war. They could have been driven ahead of assaults, like mobile sandbags, to help protect the troops that they had indirectly caused to be there. I expect too that Falkland Islanders, as well as our soldiers, would have appreciated contemplating them, possibly afflicted by incontinence, in the middle of events like Goose Green, Longdon or Tumbledown.

There was some sort of 'theme' party in the RAF Regiment Depot Officers' Mess on the Friday evening following the Argentine invasions of the Falklands and South Georgia. Most officers and their wives or partners went out of social duty, but few had much spirit for it.

It looked as if the British government was merely going to bleat to an ineffective UN. However, no one had realized what a good British soldier our lady Prime Minister was.

Most of us went to a sitting-room adjacent to the party where there was a TV set with a near constant news programme.

During 2 April, 1982, on the Falkland Islands, the Governor, sixty-seven Royal marines, twelve Royal navy Sailors and a few ex-Servicemen Islanders had held up Argentine naval and 1000-strong ground forces for five hours. They had destroyed a giant armoured amphibious Amtrac and its occupants, killed the commander of the initial assault, wounded others and had even taken some prisoners for a while.

The following day, on South Georgia 600 miles east of the

Falklands, a far smaller force of twenty-four Royal Marines and nine Royal Navy Sailors, commanded by a Lieutenant of Royal Marines, had made one of the most epic David and Goliath fights of our times. For two hours that morning they had held up an invading force of two ships and a vastly outnumbering unit of Argentine marines. They had shot down two helicopters and, by bold and skilful deployment of their single hand-held anti-tank weapon and their machine guns, had crippled a corvette and driven her from the fight.

Both the Falklands and the South Georgia parties had surrendered when finally surrounded. Beleaguered British garrisons have died to a man in the past. However, the commanders at these two events perhaps saw that the futility of a last stand would accord the flag little honour; perhaps, also, they sensed that they should survive for the revenge that was surely to follow.

As we tried to shut out the endless electric throbbing and flashing lights from the next room, our fellow Queen's Servicemen were being sent home from duty, by foreigners, via Montevideo.

Finally, it was too much. Filled with anger and shame, all the Officers and their partners left the event before it had even reached its half-way point. All, that is, except for an Education Officer and his girlfriend who carried on jigging in the racket.

William, a tall, dashing, red-curling-moustached young Officer and veteran of the Oman war and many tours to Northern Ireland, later returned to charm away and seduce the girlfriend. There was, of course, chagrin in areas of the camp's non-combatants. However, the RAF Regiment Officers were briefly cheered by the thought that someone on our side won something on that otherwise bleak night.

When a British military response finally became a possibility, I pondered if there was the slightest likelihood of another call to arms for myself. I quickly decided that there was not the remotest possibility. Combat Units go to wars, not Training Units. I was a qualified artillery and infantry officer, though slightly out-of-date on the former, but Britain had plenty of these and far younger than I. I was experienced at training, commanding in combat or working alongside native troops – the Cambodians and Montagnard in Indo-China and the Indian and Pakistan armies in Kashmir. This would not be wanted either; nor would my jungle, mountain or urban training and experience. The Falklands were almost treeless and consisted of rocky hills and boggy valleys.

I scoured my thoughts for any, even peripheral, appropriate military qualities that I might have. Staff or logistical work? No, I hated it, and was not very good at it, and there were more than enough full-timers making high-ranking careers in that sort of thing.

If one is a member of a military organization that is going to war, there is always a bit of not-selected-for-the-school-team ruefulness if one is not sent. However, I had some experiences to look back on and, unlike some of the virgin soldiers, and their mostly virgin command-ers, preparing to join the Task Force, I was rather graphically aware of the dangers to one's person during warlike events.

Such things can become even worse in retrospect as one loses the youthful, ready, and uncontemplative acceptance of events as they unfold. There just cannot be anything more sickening than suddenly destroyed or critically damaged young, precious, fellow humans, the rest of their one-and-only life taken away.

In Vietnam I saw smashed up, but still living, things arranged on a stretcher in roughly the right order, everyone staring. I can remember the upper, perhaps forty percent, of a friend who had been sawn in half by a directional mine, mercifully not in pain because of the initial numbness of shock, asking desperately with his last breath if his manhood was still intact and me saying that everything was all right.

In Kashmir there were five several-days-dead Sikh Sepoys, the tail end of a raiding party that had not made it back across the Jhelum River out of Muslim territory. The hideous disfigurement of decom-position had been enhanced by the grotesque condition and postures that vultures and wild dogs had pulled them into.

I once put a ragged piece of meat into a sandbag and labelled it with a friend's name. I once grovelled in shallow muddy water, among dead rushes, while a Dante's Inferno of flashing streaks of light flickered about the jungle night's inky blackness; the endless hammer-ing concussion of the fire exchange shook my head and hurt my ears and sinuses. I had thought that my companions had left me behind and I had snivelled in terror.

If conflict did occur in the South Atlantic, then it seemed likely that it would be 'conventional' rather than anything that I might know about. Both sides would have the most up-to-date, large-scale killing technology and the sort of open terrain in which to use it to best effect.

By and large, I felt that staying back with my lovely life in North

Yorkshire was no bad thing. I made a joke, of sorts, in the Officers'
Mess bar.

'No, I shall sit this one out!' I would say heartily to the younger
group.

Then, with my back to the bar counter which faced north, I would
raise my beer glass up at the wall in front of me in the rough direction
of the assembling Task Force on the distant south coast.

'Give 'em hell, Chaps!' I would bellow. 'With you in spirit!'

I would then roar with self-delight and to encourage laughter in the
others. They were all far too polite to let me down, even if they had
been through the not overly funny act before.

I had completely forgotten that one of the languages that I had
picked up was Spanish, indeed South American Spanish from my time
as ADC to a UN Chilean General and when eagerly paying court to
my Chilean wife. For a possible imminent involvement with Latin
Americans, it should have occurred to me that it could have a use.

PART II

To South Georgia

'The ice was here, the ice was there,
The ice was all around:
It cracked and growled, and roared and howled,
Like noises in a swound!'

The Rime Of The Ancient Mariner
by Samuel Taylor Coleridge.

(The doomed crew head into South Polar waters)

The call to arms was very much a last-minute affair. I almost missed the Task Force bus.

Having transferred to a military service that flew aeroplanes, I felt that, although I had joined its soldier corps, I really ought to learn to fly something. There was a RAF (Volunteer) Gliding School at Catterick that operated at weekends and I was fortunate enough to be officially, via application up both the flying and the RAF Regiment pillars, made a member of its Staff.

I therefore spent a large part of my off-regular-duty hours happily working about the airfield, launching, recovering and flying gliders with keen young RAF cadets and reservist Officers, Warrant Officers and NCOs. They were all local and I delighted both in their company, and the greater association with that lovely region. Soaring silently, save for the air rushing through the struts, at one to many thousand of feet above a green and varied land, is a delight almost beyond description. As an ex-paratrooper, I also felt that here was an extension of the airborne soldier; ie: the 'towed target infantry' of the Second World War.

I had asked permission of my weekday superiors to remain on duty for the long Easter weekend of 1982, as there was a large course of flying trainees in camp, and to have a couple of days off in lieu straight after the Public Holiday. They had kindly agreed.

Speculation about what might eventuate from the current Falklands situation had, of course, had a near monopoly of the airfield and crewroom conversations from Good Friday to Easter Monday.

At about a quarter to eight on the Tuesday morning I emerged from the shower in my parents' guest-room as the telephone rang downstairs. My family and I were staying with my parents on the East Sussex coast for our two days of holiday. My mother would turn the room into a sort of school dormitory. My tiny daughter had an enclosed little

23

'Goldilocks' bed so that she could not escape and make a nuisance of herself. She was staring accusingly at me through her bars.

I heard my mother's slightly disconcerted reaction when, unusually, the voice on her telephone was not that of one of her village friends.

'Er . . . oh yes. I'll call him,' she said.

Having tersely announced himself as soon as I picked up the handset, and stated that he was from a joint Service Intelligence organization, the Colonel went on, 'I have the permission of your Commandant to commandeer you for a possible role in Operation Corporate.'

It was the first time that I had heard that title and a memory of my Spanish knowledge surfaced. I knew at once that Operation Corporate was something to do with the Falklands. I tried to remember if he had said Operation Co-operate or even Corpulent.

'How soon can you get here?' He ended his short, sharp and, so far, one-sided conversation.

I pondered for a few moments and then explained to the Colonel that I had a course of new trainees arriving over the weekend and I should like to see them settled in, and, my main secondary duty being curator of my corps' museum, I had some VIP visitors to show round on Friday; so perhaps next Monday might just be a possibility. I was going to elaborate still further on the heavy, and many-sided, burdens of my responsibility, but leave no doubt that I was anxious to oblige him as soon as practicable.

He had obviously been quite enjoying himself while he let me ramble on. For the first time there was quite a human element to the voice, almost a chuckle in it.

'I am sorry that you cannot come immediately,' he said, 'but I suppose that eight o'clock tomorrow morning will have to do!'

About fifteen minutes later I departed, eating a bacon sandwich on the run.

The manner of the Colonel's last lines may not have been dramatic but the urgency of the situation, and my duty thereto, came through as clear as a bugle call – to buckle up and hurry after the column.

My membership of a fairly exclusive club, that of the multi-lingual Briton, has at times given me a very different military life. I had not learned languages through the hard effort of disciplined academic study, of course, but by the fortunate co-incidence of spending time in foreign-language-speaking company and countries when young and

24

quickly receptive. When I got older, my languages had been improved still further by what the Germans call the 'pillow method'. Despite going to schools in both England and France, I used to come bottom of the French class in England and bottom of the English class in France. Official and academically correct, rather than current, living, versions of languages tended to be taught then. I do so hope that communication, not tedious and complicated dead-rule learning, is the priority accorded to young people of today, though it is, of course sad, in principle, that the formal language structures of the centuries are being eroded in our times.

In my early Army days in Germany I used to be loaned to British Staffs or Units who were in the obviously uneasy situation of having to talk to, or work in close co-operation with, their allies.

The Senior Subaltern of my Regiment and the younger Captains gave the impression that my ability to indulge foreigners, step down to their level and actually move into their world, nationally demoted me. I became a sort of second-rate foreigner myself. It was as if, in colonial times, I had accepted a native invitation to dinner and had entered a hut! There was once a British attitude that an ability at languages should be an attribute of head waiters only. However, we should be grateful that our laziness and vanity, with a bit of back-up from the Commonwealth and the United States, has made English the international language.

The countries of Indo-China were old French colonies and I had been useful, and sometimes essential, there.

The joint Service Intelligence Centre at Ashford Camp was a hive of warlike preparation. There was not, of course, the massing of soldiery that must have been concurrently going on in Royal Marines and Airborne lines. However, battalion COs and IOs (Intelligence Officers) and Intelligence staffs were constantly reporting in and scurrying from office to office for various types of briefing.

In spite of the fact that the Argentines were some way away and people were not actually wearing face camouflage cream or leopard crawling along the grass verges, most were wearing combat kit, some even with webbing equipment. Eyes and jaws were set and lips pursed. It was obvious that the right frame of mind had already set in and was being still further engendered. The 'blast' of war had blown and the blood was being 'summoned up'.

There were some looks that suggested that it was felt that I was letting the side down by going about in a sports jacket and a pair of corduroy trousers. It was the smartest outfit that I thought that I should need while on leave. Fortunately the commander of my new Unit was not bothered, as he, of course, knew my situation.

I immediately discovered that I was to be an Interrogator, perhaps sometimes the lesser version thereof, the Field Tactical Questioner.

Even if the conflicts that I had previously attended had been of a type where chivalry to a foe could have been exercised, I cannot, of course, be certain that I should have risen to the occasion. However, I absolutely recoiled with my every instinct from becoming the type of bully and tormentor of the gallant, but now helpless, honest fighting soldier that I believed the military Interrogator to be. The Interrogator was a serpent! They were recruited from asylums for the sadistically sick in mind!

When that world was opened up to me, I saw that it was not quite what I thought. Above all, I came to understand the lifesaving and victory-hastening potential of it. Methods of Intelligence gathering are as varied as the imagination and initiative of man. However, perhaps the two most readily available to a field commander are his SAS/SBS-style special troops who move, or are inserted, among and behind his enemy and send back information – and his Interrogators.

Despite their skill and valour, the long-range special patrols can only report what they as individuals have locally discovered. However, an Interrogator has the potential to unlock minds and lay out an enemy's every detail. 'A prisoner-of-war is a walking tongue,' the Polish army have traditionally said apparently.

A Professor of Spanish from London University, who was also a Royal Auxiliary Air Force Intelligence Officer, checked my Spanish. The regular Staff of the Unit skilfully compressed the key parts of a five-week course on interrogation, tactical questioning, POW handling and related Intelligence matters to about three very full days.

The Professor of Spanish brilliantly prepared and ran my final confirmatory and testing exercise. He personally played a myriad of different ranks, roles and personality types of totally believable Argentine POWs.

They did the very best that could have been done with the material and time available. Much of the vengeance fleet had already set sail and chances to catch up with it were retreating.

There was another, and truly professional, Spanish-speaking Interrogator who had also been gathered up by the Unit. He was a Sergeant who actually was a member of the Army's Intelligence Corps, as opposed to myself who was only on a sort of attachment that, as far as I know, was never formalized. The Sergeant had spent a number of duty years in Central America and his Spanish, though cutely English-accented, was technically faultless.

The other member of our eventual team, or unit, was another highly qualified Spanish-speaking Interrogator/Tactical Questioner who was already on a vessel that had started on the 8,000-mile voyage towards the ultimate test for we three novices in real terms, and, indeed, for most other Task Force appointments.

This member was a RAF Flight Sergeant of highly sophisticated electronic surveillance, interception and other related skills. He had had our, not dissimilar, but more basic, physical and interface specializations added to his abilities. He had been an Instructor at the Interrogation School and was, therefore, the superior in skills and effect.

The Flight Sergeant was a pure-blooded Englishman who, because of his father's work location, had grown up in Central America. He was totally bilingual. We could have put him in an Argentine uniform and infiltrated him as a fifth columnist.

My Spanish had been acquired without ever having been to a Spanish-speaking country, though I had spent time in a small diplomatic community when Aide de Camp to a Chilean UN General. Even during the year before I met my wife, I was in the presence of exclusively Spanish-speaking young ladies. Necessity is the master of, probably all, invention I fear. I could read anything and, not very grammatically, write and say anything, particularly things of a romantic or improperly suggestive nature, in Spanish. I could be witty and crack jokes and I had a very thorough knowledge of South American slang and crudities; this last inadmirable attribute was to prove to be a surprise gem for my future role and relationship with the young men of that sub-continent.

Although we gained occasional and brief peripheral assistance from random, untrained, slightly Spanish-speaking British military passers-by once war had been joined, we three, newly met up, were the 'Combined British Forces Interrogation Unit' for the duration of hostilities.

No one ever got round to typing us in on the Force's Order of Battle, so officially we never existed and had no entitlement to ammunition, rations, a radio set or any form of logistical or administrative support. However, it goes without saying, of course, that officers and soldiers on the ground, once they had realized our role in the scheme of things, gave every assistance they could, even, on occasions, to the slight prejudice of their own Units.

It was unfortunate, albeit unintentioned, that a magnificent POW Handling Unit was disembarked on to Port Stanley Public Jetty a few days after the cessation of hostilities and when there were only a few POWs left. It was commanded by a Major, had commissioned Oxbridge linguists, a computer and actually had POW guards of its own. They had also had a preparatory training exercise in the United Kingdom before embarking, using a whole British infantry batallion to simulate Argentine POWs.

During the fighting, therefore, the 12,500 land combatants of the Argentine force who survived had the insult of being dealt with only by us 'amateur' and, officially unsupported, three.

An Interrogator is meant to be as a Consultant Surgeon. Lesser specialized persons select necessary cases, complete the ground work and give the unique appointment as much information as possible that he may then have the best chance of achieving the desired result. The Interrogator, like the medical specialist, has an office, without distractions, to allow maximum concentration on the intricate study.

My endless battle throughout the campaign was to prevent my 'specialists' being used by the ignorant on POW processing, clerical work, International Red Cross Spanish form-filling and even POW guarding.

'We've got lots of prisoners for you to sort out,' Majors and Lieutenant-Colonels would usually say, as we joined them at their recent battlefield, and my heart would sink. They always looked pleased and relieved to see us because they thought that we conveniently 'got rid of' POWs.

I would usually suggest that he, probably assisted by his IO, 'sorted out' his POWs in accordance with his Unit's Standing Orders or British Forces' pamphlets on the subject, let me know what IRs (intelligence requirements) he would like for his future operations, and that these particular POWs might have, and my unit would try to get them.

Reactions varied; a few, after muttering about insubordination, a lack of co-operation, a total ignorance of infantry operations and their Unit's current difficulties, abandoned us to it. Others met us a little or larger part along the way.

None of us would have got a place on the transport going South if the CO of our parent Intelligence Unit had turned out to be the conservative that he superficially appeared to be and not the inspired man of high principle, great moral courage and loyalty to the Nation that he in fact was. He put his career on the line to right a wrong that he knew, if allowed to continue unchecked, would prejudice the Falklands Task Force.

The problem no doubt was that the last memory of when British forces had independently fought a regular foreign foe ended in 1945. In the Korean War of the 1950s Britain was part of a multi-national UN force and there were South Koreans and Western Chinese to speak to communist prisoners. Friendly locals, or local colonial soldiers, could interrogate hostiles during the post-WW2 British withdrawal-from-Empire conflicts. The British forces had not needed integral Interrogators.

Thus the moment, on or about 30 April, 1982, that an officer of the Argentine submarine *Santa Fé* was brought to me in the conference room of RFA *Tidespring*, as we returned from South Georgian waters, was the first time a British military Interrogator went into, or was needed to go into, action for thirty-seven years. Such a period can put things out of mind.

Modern British forces train scientifically and well; their record proves this. However, all too frequently upon positions being 'captured', even in the largest formation's training exercises, the 'enemy' cease pretending to be dead or standing with their hands up and are returned to their controlling organization. They have usually been borrowed from a different command and, if they are to give the impression of being an entire opposing 'army', they must be shuttled around to provide every part of the 'goodies' front a realistic-sized force might come up against. Their time cannot be wasted. It would also not be the best use of expensive and ever-lessening training time if they were retained for boring POW compound-minding practices and the slow and drawn-out business of interrogation preparation and processing.

It seemed, therefore, that the British military hierarchy had just forgotten about, or at least not fully envisaged, what happened after a battle was won and the many implications and facets of POWs.

Our Colonel, I am sure for the first time in his life, did unthinkable military things. Via the telephone, he broke chains of command and went straight to the top. He spoke to Ministers and influential personalities. He endured senior abuse, threats and, worst of all, supercilious, ignorant sarcasm. However, they were dealing with a bulldog whose hold, in the cause of duty, could not be shaken off. The obvious truth of his message finally got through and, to be fair, once it did get through, it got through well. In the end there was great support from the highest downwards, but the eleventh hour had already struck.

I believe, and certainly hope, that our Colonel never suffered professionally in any way for his high sense of responsibility. We, his men, certainly saved lives in the conflict to come by discovering what lay ahead for our advancing forces and we may have helped fractionally to hasten victory and end the killing. Anything that we did was only possible because of a man on a telephone in a Portakabin office who was faithful enough to brush to one side nearly thirty years of painstaking work, difficult inching up the career ladder, his status and the financial security of his family.

A large military force is lacking an essential commodity if it sets out without people who can talk to those it must fight and who are also trained to make several uses of their ability. The only linguists listed on Service computers were those speaking Eastern European and Asian languages in case World War Three against the communist empires should crop up, so the Colonel told the authorities that he had made an informal trawl round the three forces, as comprehensive as time would allow, and had accumulated just three sufficiently proficient Spanish speakers. One was trained, and on his Staff, and could go with the very first elements of the Task Force and the other two, which included myself, were being prepared and would be ready shortly. He was finally told to get his 'Unit' South by any means that he could engineer.

Our fabulous Commanding Officer further lectured the no doubt gagging top brass! If the recapture of South Georgia, as a prelude to a main campaign, was envisaged, then, although the Argentines there might have no knowledge of the dispositions on the Falklands, critical general information could be gained from them: equipment in service, their state of training, their quality, their morale and overall intentions.

'Two days!' the Colonel said to the Sergeant and myself as soon as we had raced into his office, following his shout into the corridor where we had been lurking and listening, and stood at attention. He looked tired but there was a gleam of triumph, almost emotion, in his eyes.

'I give you two days to say your goodbyes,' he continued. 'Then I expect you know where you're going.'

It was a statement, not a question. There had been enough reliable intimation. We knew exactly where we were going.

'Pick up your travel warrants from the office,' he roared after our respectful but fast-fleeing forms.

I drove my family back to North Yorkshire and my two days were as idyllic as ever in that place and in that company. They were weekdays, so I delivered and collected my young son from the village school and wheeled my daughter to and from her little crèche.

'*Te gusta el colegio?*' I asked her as we returned one lunchtime. She still spoke only Spanish and I was certain that she must love the pretty hall with its toys, games and kind lady supervisors.

She slowly shook her little sullen and bowed head and then struggled round in her pushchair to stare at me over its back. Her expression indicated that it was necessary to confirm that someone so stupid could exist.

'What happens if you die or something?' my wife asked casually as I prepared to leave for the waiting military transport to Darlington railway station.

I explained, and outlined, that because of insurance policies, a Forces' benevolent fund that I contributed to and various considerations that were built into the system for 'war widows', she would be better off than if I stayed alive.

She accepted the situation. She was an army daughter. She had even been a soldier. She had never worn a uniform, of course, but then the majority of those who do, and have long 'military' careers in and generous pensions from regular standing armed forces, never are or never get the chance.

During the 1973 rebellion in Chile against President Allende, who had evolved into a Marxist autocrat, communist militia, including Soviet surrogate Cubans, came to murder the wives and children of the rebel military in their housing area. The regular officers and soldiers, including my wife's father, were away fighting the main communist forces.

My wife's family home was on a sharp corner position and was both strategic and fortifiable. My wife's mother gathered as many dependants as possible and everyone crammed onto the floors at the ground level as the communists held the surrounding heights and rooftops and constantly raked the upper parts of the building with gunfire. A young Chilean soldier, who had been working in the housing area, joined them and brought with him two machine guns and a good quantity of ammunition.

The large corner kitchen gave good fields of fire on two sides and the soldier and Irma, the country girl housemaid who turned out to be a dead shot, kept the communist killers at bay from their respective windows.

My wife, who was then fifteen, and her fourteen-year-old sister squatted on the floor of the bullet-riddled room rapidly breaking open ammunition boxes, loading Bren magazines, passing them forward to the maid and the soldier and taking back the empties for refilling.

The families had several days with little sleep and the maid and the soldier had none. It seemed to them that they must be doomed. However, a relief force that included husbands and fathers finally fought through to them.

One or two British service wives, particularly 'academic' officers' wives with no military background or concept of their war role to 'keep the home fires burning' and who had modern marriages, where husbands additionally do some of the wife's chores, did not do well during the Falklands War. There were tiny deputations to the popular press, military and government offices. Their point, apparently, was that they should not be denied their partners and only single men should go away for prolonged periods. Some were used by the tiny stop-the-rescue movement. This included street mobs and left-wing socialist politicians such as Judith Hart and Anthony Wedgwood Benn.

Judith Hart is only remembered for unceasing vitriolic criticism of Prime Minister Margaret Thatcher. Anthony Wedgwood Benn has proletarianized into 'Tony Benn'.

'You're the man of the house now,' I said jokingly to my son. 'Take care of your mother and sister.'

*

'A large ashtray at the dead centre of the Atlantic' was how a veteran Royal Navy Officer, who met us on the runway, described Ascension Island. He had anchored off the place once or twice in the past. He was one of the first of the tri-Service people to arrive and start activating the place as a military transit base. Reactivate is probably more correct as, in the days when the Royal Navy was the policeman of the seas, the island must have been a critical place – the only source of fresh water, goats' meat, vegetables and fruit for at least five hundred miles in any direction. The imposing eighteenth century style of the little administrative capital of Georgetown indicated a past significance.

The traditional Royal Navy description was certainly accurate concerning the coastal areas of the island – nothing but hills of coke stretched around and above us as we stood on Wideawake airfield. However, just beyond, at the centre of the island were green bamboo-covered mountains and the fenced-off offices and dwellings, where the ubiquitous wandering and devouring goats could not go, had court-yards fringed with lush tropical shrubs.

Our party of six had been rapidly formed at the Ministry of Defence in London and at the joint-Service Intelligence centre. We had a large, and hugely bearded, Royal Navy Lieutenant Commander from the Intelligence Staff who was the outfit's 'ringmaster'; 'controller' was probably the correct title. There were three equipment experts and two Spanish-speakers: the Sergeant and myself.

The equipment experts consisted of two naval sub-mariners, whose field was undersea warfare, and a Lieutenant Colonel of the Royal Engineers, whose study was the heavier catergories of foreign military kit: missiles, armoured vehicles, etc.

The experts would decide the areas in which they would like enquiry to be made of the South Georgia Argentinians, when and if they were captured; our controller would select likely subjects and administra-tively stage-manage all aspects of the process and the Sergeant and I would try to get what was wanted.

The Royal Navy experts were an entertaining and diametrically opposite pair. The more senior was a Commander in what, I imagine, is the Royal Navy's traditional school – a clean-shaven, incredibly distinguished and serious countenance and most thoughtful, precise and articulate speech. Despite his calling, he had a quaintly inno-cent, country clergyman, aspect. One felt that he must have locked himself in his cabin during stopovers in places like Port Said when young.

His partner, a young Lieutenant, was the very personification of the ever more technological armed forces of the future. He had a razor-sharp intellect and wit. He regularly, but with such skill and subtlety as to be totally within the bounds of subordination, made unmerciful fun of his two serious Service superiors.

The Army Colonel was an obviously dedicated, highly knowledge-able, urbane and quiet man.

Shortly after our arrival in the heat of Ascension Island the Royal Navy Commander appeared in a pair of calf-length shorts that must have been turn-of-the-century issue. One could probably have taken several paces before the shorts would have moved. We three younger members of the party were aghast and I am sure that the well-being of some of the United States Air Force and communications personnel, who leased part of the base, was put at risk by them.

The walk of those who came suddenly upon our group would immediately, and inconspicuously, speed up. Their ankles positively twinkled. With shining eyes set determinedly ahead, as they could obviously not trust themselves if they took a second glance, lips tightly compressed and scarlet, bulging, near-exploding cheeks, they raced to the nearest office or storeroom where they could hurl themselves about.

The Lieutenant suggested to me that if any prisoners-of-war were unco-operative, I should threaten them with being made to wear the Commander's shorts for a while. However, we finally decided that such inhuman cruelty would unquestionably get one put on trial later for war crimes.

The part of the Task Force that was to retake South Georgia had set off days earlier and we had to try and catch it up. A giant Chinook helicopter, of the type that I well remembered from the Vietnam War, just over ten years previously, was prepared for us. Most of the aircraft's interior was filled by a gigantic extra fuel tank. There was just sufficient space left at the front for the two pilots, we six and a large inflatable liferaft. This was to be an epic, one-way, ultimate Chinook-range journey to the cold waters.

If the force was not found, or a deck landing not achieved, then we had to ditch into the sea. Even with our incredible modification, sufficient aviation fuel could not possibly be carried to do otherwise.

We rose out over the equatorial sea into the very earliest lightening of our first Ascension Island dawn. Our destination was some tiny specks of fellow humanity floating on the centre of a vast, cold ocean several climatic zones away.

Less than twenty-four hours earlier we had left Brize Norton on an RAF Tristar. The aircraft had been packed with yet more Royal Marines who were being sent South. They would no doubt meet up with their ships at Ascension.

At about the half-way point of that journey we had a brief stop in Senegal. Under a friendly international agreement, some RAF Movement personnel were temporarily stationed there. A group of them came over to the airport parking area where we all shuffled about, studying the endless baked earth mounds and shrivelled shrubs of Central Africa, for a chat.

It was known that the breathtaking beaches of this former French colony were a popular holiday resort for the well-heeled of France. There were envious murmurings and some winks and nudges from the aircraft's passengers about the successes that the youthful clean-cut RAF men must be having with the considerably exposed female tourists. However, the Air Movers told us sadly that the French women came to experience native parts and had no interest in things similar to those at home.

As there had been no significant disputes in the central Atlantic for many decades, Ascension Island must have become very tranquil. However, in the space of two weeks, it had been transformed into a crowded platform from which British combat power readied itself for the bound southwards.

War, transport and technical ships lay at anchor all around. Military aircraft: fighters, tankers, transporters and helicopters filled the waiting bays of its once flying-club-like airfield. Transit troops were housed in rows of every conceivable type of military tent, in a constant suspension of volcanic dust, between the edges of the airfield and the high-tide mark.

Military people milled busily about in every area of the greater airbase. Heavily laden store-carrying vehicles, like low railless trains, moved among them. The constant sounds of shooting practice, single shots and automatic bursts of several calibres, regularly crashed out of adjacent valleys.

The island's normally few regular inhabitants – United States satellite and communications personnel and the USAF, who moved them about, the British civil servants and their families and the St Helena Islanders, who did the simpler administrative work – either kept out of the way of all this unwonted bustle or were delighted by the interesting and unusual aspect of it all and enthusiastically lent a hand.

The St Helena Islanders were certainly a valuable asset. They looked like Africans who were about one quarter British, they spoke as if educated at an English private school, had good manners that disappeared long ago from even the supposedly most cultured of mainland British society and set about every task, no matter how menial, enthusiastically, cheerfully and efficiently.

On every occasion that I started to walk the mile or so from Georgetown to the airfield, the St Helenian-run rubbish truck approached from behind. It slowed and, before I knew what had happened, several sets of powerful arms had reached down and swept me up from the track to the centre of their beaming group amongst the refuse. It was inconceivable to them to pass by a fellow being who could be assisted in any way.

The wives and daughters of the British governors, who became known as the 'memsahibs', wearing pretty English summer dresses and straw hats, thrust a very welcome mug of tea and a piece of exquisite home-made cake into the hands of every Serviceman who wandered into the picturesque little central square of Georgetown.

Exotic and unusual, scorching hot but with fresh breezes, Ascension Island could have been one of the greatest holiday paradises on earth – had it not been for its sea.

The moment you walked into its shallows, powerful water hands, that reached out from the vastness of the central Atlantic, closed round your legs and tried to draw you to its source. It is the strongest undercurrent I have ever encountered. You immediately knew that you must not take your feet from the seabed or go in above your knees. The inshore area was patrolled by shoals of a type of sea pirhana fish and voracious sharks. Every seventh breaker was a disproportionate giant that could either drown you or cast you to the invisible leviathan that desired you in the depths.

The post-war island garrison personnel are forbidden by military order from swimming anywhere, except in their new swimming pool or on the one protected and supervised beach.

Despite the fact that everyone was so busy, assistance and support to our group was given a priority. It was gratifying evidence that our office-bound but gallant Colonel's exceptional efforts had produced significant results.

Men had worked constantly for several days and nights to convert our helicopter and two of the best of the much-needed RAF Chinook pilots had been allocated to us.

The more senior was a bold-moustached and chirpy ex-Royal Australian Air Force pilot. His unbelievable flying skill and strong personal qualities were to prove critical to our risky journey. I wondered if he were a fellow Vietnam veteran. I never got the chance to ask him. I know of only one other old Indo-China soldier who also served in the Falklands campaign. He was an ex-Rifleman of the Royal Australian Regiment who had become a SNCO in the British Army's Intelligence Corps.

There was endless wrinkled sea below us. We saw it white and twinkling at dawn, we saw it blue, warm and sunny on an early tropical morning and we saw it go a darker blue and emanate a chill as the day wore on. By early evening the sea was grey, rough and cold and our fuel was almost ended.

It seemed as if we had never known a time when we had not sat in a great tube, on hard seats, while two giant rotors thudded overhead and our world unceasingly shook in rhythm.

The Australian Squadron Leader still grinned at anyone who caught his eye as if he had not a care in the world. He spoke to the ship that we headed for occasionally; unfortunately it was always to report, 'We do not have you visual yet'.

It was getting dark and our, by that time, desultory conversation dried up. We all knew what must happen, and apprehension as icy as the sea below started to grip.

'There she is,' the Squadron leader suddenly said in a matter-of-fact tone. 'The old *Tidespring*'.

He later told us that he had been turning his head to us to say, 'Partially inflate your life jackets, tighten your seatbelts and brace yourselves,' when he had spotted the RFA *Tidespring* on the forward horizon.

Our worried feelings were not to be immediately ended. The giant helicopter had to be landed on the deck of the tanker, in fast-fading light, as she pitched in a freezing choppy sea. I was also concerned about her helicopter landing pad. Though there was a white circle painted on the sternmost deck, it looked as if it was intended for the smaller Royal Navy helicopters only.

Our wonderful pilots inched us down, revolved, adjusted, raised a little when necessary and, although a wheel might tap a piece of superstructure with a sound metallic clang, the two vast rotors were kept clear of the forest of electronic paraphernalia that covered the top of the vessel. Minute by heart-stopping minute, they tucked us in. On the only configuration possible, they finally brought us softly to rest. Our wheels seemed to be protruding slightly over the edges of the rolling deck.

Long-haired merchant seamen, in filthy overalls, rushed about us and lashed the awkward-shaped flying machine to the deck with a speed, efficiency and devotion that could not have been bettered by the most pressed and gleaming team in the Royal Navy.

Having shut down the strong and faithful engines, the RAF pilots, in their usual all-in-a-day's-work style, sprang out and started cracking jokes with the ship's officers and crew. We, the passengers, could only remain limply in our seats for a while, gaping with awe both at them and our recent experience.

Along the dimly lit corridor a man slowly approached my 'office'. An armed Royal Marine had pointed out where he was to go with a strong, straight and motionless arm and forefinger. Silently, and outwardly without emotion, the man had obeyed.

The last man in his situation would probably have been a German or Japanese in 1945, on the last occasion that a foreign regular military foe came before a British Interrogator.

This was the first 'enemy' of this war whom I had encountered at close quarters. He was young, of medium height and strong, athletic build. He wore a light-blue denim military-style shirt with darker blue denim trousers, similar to the working uniform of the Royal Navy. However, it was the moustache that gave him away. Queen Victoria personally decided that she wished Her Sailors to be either clean-shaven or fully bearded; there were to be no half-way stages.

The moustache, and his hair, were streaked blond, probably because his life was spent in the fresh air, on the sea, in sun, wind and saltspray. Nonetheless, his dark Latin eyes and the Spanish surname that I had at the top of a piece of paper on my desk left no doubt of who and what he was.

'Ardilla' — sadly I forget her surname these days but I think it had an Italian sound — was my very first girlfriend when I was a youth in London. She was an Argentinian student of English and was a little older than myself. I think she gave me up because my innocence made me less generally effective than she might have wished. Strangely, the memory and vision of her had returned to me with incredible clarity for the first time in about twenty-five years, from the moment that we brought the Argentine prisoners-of-war on board.

I fervently prayed that henceforward, in a totally different area, I might be highly effective with every Argentine that I met.

I greeted the Argentine Navy Lieutenant with a beaming smile, a courteous Spanish pleasantry, partially stood up and waved him to the chair that faced me on the other side of my desk. The Royal Navy, non-Spanish-speaking Lieutenant and undersea warfare expert, who sat to one side of me, silently did likewise.

Obviously there was guile behind our behaviour but there was sincerity too. The Argentine Officer had, to our knowledge, done nothing dishonourable during the two rounds of fighting on South Georgia except follow his government's flawed philosophy. He also seemed a pretty decent sort of chap, all things considered. He smiled and sat down without speaking.

I asked him, in Spanish, if he spoke English. He politely replied that he had very little knowledge of that language. This was highly unlikely. His speech, manners and position indicated top-quality education and English is the main second language of Argentinians. It was also probable that, as an Officer in their Navy, he would have attended courses in Britain or the United States. However, I said chirpily, 'No importa' (never mind).

The Intelligence Corps Sergeant had been allocated to the Argentine Army personnel and I to their Navy. He was concurrently sitting in another improvised 'office', the foreign land military equipment Lieutenant-Colonel at his side, and would be talking to an Argentine Marine or Special Forces soldier.

I wondered if Interrogators in times past had ever had the sort of difficulties and inhibiting factors cast in their path that he and I had. The Argentinians were not, of course, a problem. It was the British Government and the International Red Cross who had, albeit with worthy intentions, somewhat sabotaged us. Our government apparently hoped that, despite the fact that the bell had clanged, the seconds were out of the ring and the contestants had been raining blows on each other, a peaceful settlement might still be possible via the various international arbitration attempts that were going on.

Grim-faced, our Lieutenant Commander controller had told us while we were on Ascension Island that he had received a copy of Ministerial (or Prime Ministerial?) signal stating that there was to be no interrogation of Argentine South Georgia POWs. However, it also reportedly said that as much information as possible was to be obtained! We unsavoury Interrogators were not to sully the national image at what might be a critical time, but we were to do our job.

Three officials of the International Red Cross had been helicoptered on to the *Tidespring* as she returned from the recapture of South Georgia. She had prisoners-of-war on board and they, of course, had their international duty of ensuring that they were being correctly treated.

It occurred to all levels of command the zealous reaction that could be expected from the noble, serious-minded, humanitarian and neutral Swiss if they discovered that interrogation was going on. We were, therefore, told that on no account were we to get caught doing the job that we were 'not to do'.

Also in the helicopter that brought the International Red Cross officials on board had been Royal Navy and British Ministry of Defence and Legal civilian members of a Court of Inquiry that was to investigate the truly tragic circumstances of the shooting of an Argentine Navy Petty Officer prisoner by a Royal Marine guard.

The Court would be held during the voyage back to Ascension. They had heard that there were Spanish-speakers on board and so, as such men seemed difficult to find, they had not brought any of their own. The Sergeant and I would translate for them!

If it had not been for the miraculous coincidence of a Royal Navy officer being accidentally discovered on the *Tidespring* who was a reasonable Spanish linguist and could look after the Court then the interrogation that was 'not to be done' would have collapsed.

The not-inconsiderable obstacles had obviously given me cause for thought. I had already been sufficiently worried about the alien military ground that I was about to tread after nearly twenty years as a conventional soldier.

Without mentioning anything to the Interrogation establishment, as they were probably fairly conservative about their art, I decided to tailor my training to the campaign, and the unusual and changing phases that it looked as if it were going to go through, and the national character that I believed the enemy had from my general observations of South Americans and my reading of Argentinians.

Our current philosophy on military interrogation has come about through the experience and study of this century's wars, both our own and other nation's, and the purists do believe in a hard and fast set of rules, which, in the event, I was forced to bend.

The two main obstacles to fully effective interrogation in both theatres of the South Atlantic war, in my opinion, were a lack of time and a lack of conducive facilities. For example it soon became obvious that the First and Second World Wars were going to be long, large and slow-moving. There would be time to plan a comprehensive Interrogation campaign. There would be time to select and prepare the best subjects carefully and time for the Interrogators subtly to implement the intricate subterfuges that they had gleaned were the way to extract voluntary or involuntary information from the prisoners. The fact that there was not great urgency allowed time for the setting-up of properly designed and manned Interrogation Centres where the Interrogator, free of the distraction of having to dodge the passing ordnance, could concentrate single-mindedly on nothing but getting the IRs demanded. Not all, no doubt, but a number of military Interrogators in those times must have been in the ideal 'specialist consultant' role! Had dear old 'pie-in-the-sky' World War Three, that gave countless peacetime military careerists such a materially wonder-ful life for over forty years, ever happened, there is no reason to suppose that Interrogation could not have been as in the former two wars.

However, the British side of the Falklands War rolled forward at a fast pace. Troops preparing during the day to go into battle that night needed critical information from prisoners taken a few hours earlier. The Interrogators had to be near those they served and so the 'interrogation centre' might be a cold and damp Falklands farm outbuilding. More likely, however, the Argentinian would be invited to select a rock or a segment of peat bog to sit on and the Interrogator's technical back-up would be a notebook and a biro kept in a wet combat smock pocket. One would desperately attempt, while keeping the POW forthcoming by any means, to achieve subsequently decipherable notes as the constant ferocious gale and the stinging rain or sleet did their worst with your pages.

The Commanding Officer of our joint service Intelligence Unit had, in good faith and quite understandably at the time, said that my team and I would operate from a ship's cabin; somewhere safe but not too far from the forward troops. His dedicated and skilled Staff had prepared a magnificent 'battle box' for us. It contained every possible type of stationery item, wall-charts for listing and plotting the progress and movement of POWs, reference works and technological equipment.

My past experience of life on the ground, once the fighting starts, had made me wary even before I left Britain. As soon as I encountered the South Georgia and Falkland Islands POW situations, my thoughts and fears were confirmed; we were going to have to tailor official training and improvise on the spot.

Sadly, we never saw our wondrous 'battle box' again. It followed us faithfully to sub-Antarctic waters in the hold of a warship. But my 'unit' became a land force from the moment of its arrival at San Carlos.

As soon as I got back after the war, I telephoned my way through an exhausting chain of Royal Navy Supply Officers and Army Quartermasters to try and ensure that the box returned safely home. I do so hope that it did, and was not just plundered by passing servicemen, as it was so scientifically and painstakingly prepared and, if circumstances had been as they should, would have made all the difference in the world.

The Latin character, of which the Argentines have an extreme form, is so pronounced as to be fairly well known: volatile, emotional, cunning and generous, and mercurial, yet fragile; egos that weld together to make proud, demonstratively patriotic and assertive nations.

With time, skilful interrogation can probably erase national person-alities and reduce all to the two basic types of POW – those who talk and those who do not. It was because of the lack of time, therefore, that the Argentines never met, in myself, an obvious Interrogator. My SNCOs, I believe, also did more or less likewise. Those whom Argentine POWs did meet individually were several easy-to-talk-to types. If in a short time I had become quickly obvious as an Interrogator, their loyalty as a serviceman and their alarms and defences would have been aroused.

A sudden or aggressive attempt to get to a point, because there was insufficient time for an innocuous-seeming lead-in, produces fear and anger and, in the case of the Argentines, they would erupt into the same old national propaganda and any hope of success, with that particular subject, was irrevocably ended.

The ex-South Georgia Argentines encountered a frightfully jolly, incredibly chatty, rather simple, easily impressed and marginally competent eccentric British 'official' of some kind and the Falklands' Argentines encountered the same type, except that by then he was a Captain who just happened to be passing by and just could not resist the chance to practise his bit of Spanish!

'Finest language in the world . . . Visited a few parts of Central and South America, sadly not Argentina. I hear that it's a super place!' And so forth.

This deception and misuse of honest men, even if they were my country's enemies at the time, was not honourable; and, though I am proud of the just result our Force achieved, I think of my part with sadness today.

Yet the way I set about things, I think and hope, additionally saved Argentine conscience and honour in what was mercifully to be a short campaign, free of either intense or lasting hatred. The roles I played enabled any POW who was forthcoming with me to believe, and say to his comrades, that a fellow of no consequence had just chatted to him, even if an inkling of suspicion had at the time, or subsequently, crossed his mind. This may sound irrelevant, but, of the few men who go to fight for their country, most will go only once and it will be the most dramatic memory of a lifetime. I am glad that I was able to do my job and, hopefully, not give any worthy men a lasting inner heartache because of a false belief that they failed in their ultimate national duty in any way. My style may also have stopped the whisper 'Interrogator' from sweeping through the vast communal POW holding locations from whence I had to collect, and then return, those I spoke with.

Before meeting the South Georgia POWs I had made up, and had typed and run off in many copies, a 'repatriation form' to provide something to distract the Argentinians, and myself, and to give us a believable object to talk around.

However, I fear that the almost comic British official filled them in very marginally. He was forever being distracted to crack an infantile joke, ask if it was really true that Buenos Aires had the biggest or best in something or the other, ask if it was really true that the Argentine

43

Navy had really purchased the latest in this or that type of equipment from France, West Germany or the USA and how on earth did they deploy such advanced technology. It would be far too complicated for we thick 'gringos' and especially myself! (Rounding off with British 'Old School' laughter, an unprincipled impersonation of the RAF Regiment Training Wing Second-in-Command!)

The first Argentine submariner Navy Lieutenant was followed by most of the other junior officers, some technical Petty Officers of the *Santa Fe* and, at the end of a near twenty-four-hour day, a senior officer from the submarine. Mercifully at this point our kindly but unstinting controller saw that the Royal Navy Lieutenant and I could no longer talk or write properly and told us to get a few hours' sleep. The Royal Marine guards secured any waiting POWs back in their helicopter hangar accommodation and we rolled from our chairs onto the office carpet and sank into instant, deep and, curiously, not uncomfortable sleep.

Without the opportunity, or permission, for proper, in-depth interrogation, we were not able to get all the detail that we, and the nation, would have wished. However, for my part, I believe that I was able to present to the Admiralty a thorough general picture of Argentine undersea warfare from which their specialists could 'guesti-mate' the minutae: types of submarine in service and where they all were at that moment, the methods their submarines used to escape detection, the methods used to escape destruction, types of torpedos in service, an idea of Argentine seamanship skills (considerable) and their sub-marine tactics. Sea mines (anti-ship, anti-submarine and bottom) are the other aspects of undersea warfare and here, too, I was able to discover types in service, policy and methods of laying.

For several very long-seeming days the Sergeant and I had carefully inched our way along with our human and, therefore, totally unpre-dictable material. The Sergeant, deceptively pedantic, bespectacled and clerical, was unrelenting. I may not have done much for the national image but every one of the dozen or so *Santa Fe* crew members I had 'interviewed' had spoken with me to a greater or lesser extent and we had got most of what was wanted, and in the way that was wanted.

I had not talked to the Captain of the *Santa Fe*, as it had been correctly assumed that he, no doubt being the oldest and wisest on board, would immediately have smelled a rat. The Court of Inquiry had conveniently, but unintentionally, distracted both him and the officials of the International Red Cross from our activities. However, by about our third day of interrogation, he had either heard something in the POW accommodation or had noticed that different Officers and Petty Officers kept being spirited away for a few hours at a time and had put two and two together. He had, therefore, given his men a quick and compressed lecture on Resistance to Interrogation. Thus, we suddenly found that we were getting nothing but the Big Three: name, rank and serial number. Fortunately, by that time, we had probably gained all that we were going to get anyway.

The language of undersea warfare was, of course, a thing that I, a land soldier, had no idea of and so I had to do a great deal of pre-interrogation study. (An anti-submarine torpedo decoy is '*un blanco/ senuelo de torpedo antisubmarino*', not a difficult or inobvious name but not the sort of thing one has on the tip of the tongue for everyday use.) I even learned quite a bit about undersea warfare. Its varied aspects and inventiveness are fascinating but horrendous.

A few weeks later I was to be on a Royal Navy surface craft during an air raid. The orders for us soldiers on these occasions were that we should lie on our narrow many-tiered bunks, in our tiny cabins, having first screwed shut all hatches between ourselves and the open air several decks above. The visions of what might ensue if that floating metal anthill was holed was the stuff of the very worst nightmares – struggling with a buckled and unopenable hatch while seawater quickly rises over your chin and nostrils! After that experience, therefore, and in view of what I by then knew from the submariners, being on the receiving end of hostile projectiles while actually *under* the water was too ghastly to be thinkable.

I cannot know if the information I gained was of benefit, as, apart from the Argentine mining of Port Stanley harbour, there was only one brief, but spectacular, incident of undersea warfare during the South Atlantic War. The British submarine *Conqueror* torpedoed and sank the Argentine cruiser *General Belgrano* on Sunday, 2 May, 1982. 350 sailors died and about 650, some horrifically burned, took to the mountainous icy sea, of 60mph gales and 18ft waves, in liferafts. More lives were lost subsequently as rafts overturned. After a terrible night and day on that merciless ocean, most Argentine survivors were recovered by other vessels of their fleet.

Though HMS *Conqueror* triumphantly flew a pirate flag as she sailed back into her base, the mood of the British nation was one of sadness that such an action had become necessary. We, who were on that same sea, looked imaginatively at it and were moved.

The sub-Antarctic elements had plagued the British recapture of South Georgia at almost every phase. The sea there is not like anything that I have seen before. The waves do not undulate, they seem to remain in colossal permanent grey freezing mountains that move slowly and ominously about. Later in the war I saw huge British aircraft-carriers smash into them and shudder along their length. An officer of the troopship *Canberra* told me that, one night when he was Officer-of-the-Watch, they were climbing up the slope of a water mountain when the slope became so long and steep that *Canberra* started to slide backwards. If it had continued she could have driven her great stern under the water and been in grave danger. Fortunately, by some rapid and skilful ship handling, he managed to avert the disaster. He told me that he had never encountered anything like it before in a long career at sea.

A great freak wave had hit RFA *Tidespring* a sledgehammer blow to her side, on the way down, and had buckled her superstructure. The weather had also defeated the first British attack. Special Air Service troops pre-positioned for assault from the Fortuna Glacier had to be recovered after a night on the ice despite their renowned endurance and regular Arctic training in North Norway. Conditions so terrible just could not have been envisaged. Two helicopters that went to their rescue were suddenly enveloped in a totally blinding blizzard and crashed. An incredibly brave Fleet Air Arm pilot flew his helicopter back into the horror, overloaded his aircraft with the survivors and their kit and made it back to a British vessel.

Two other would-be approaches towards the objectives by groups of Royal Marine and Army Special Forces, in small assault boats, fared no better. The engines of one group failed and the powerful winds and surging currents started to sweep them away into the vastness of the Arctic Ocean. They would never have been seen again. Mercifully, by superhuman effort and a bit of luck, they managed to get hold on the tip of the very last finger of land before the open sea. Chunks of ice, hurled by wind blast from a glacier, rained down on the second group and started to sink their craft. They too had to be recovered.

The little force, both ships and men, had at this point seemed somewhat scattered and momentum appeared to have ground to a halt. Of the three vessels, RFA *Tidespring* had landed her troops and had been ordered out to sea and the two warships (destroyers HMS *Antrim* and HMS *Plymouth*) were also out at sea meeting up with another RN vessel, that was giving wider area defence, to replace lost kit. The land force was spread about in a number of packets; not all were where they, and the Force Commander, wanted them to be.

However, before there could have been even the slightest risk of any malaise setting in, a rapid turn of events had occurred.

Just over a day after the Force's bleakest hour, on 25 April, 1982, a Wessex helicopter from the returned warships had spotted the Argentine submarine *Santa Fe* on the surface near the main South Georgia base of Grytviken. The helicopter immediately attacked with depth charges. Other helicopters quickly swarmed in and fired a missile, an anti-submarine torpedo and machine guns.

Holed in several places, notably the conning tower and the tail fin, leaking oil and pouring smoke, the *Santa Fe* had beached alongside the jetty of the British Antarctic Survey base at King Edward's Point. We discovered, during our later 'interrogation', that the event had considerably shocked and demoralized the Argentine garrison.

The initiative, at this point, had been taken by a dynamic SAS Major. Knowing that action following quickly on the heels of this Argentine setback would be advantageous, he had gained permission from the Royal Navy Force Commander to assault the main base of Grytviken as soon as was possible with every soldier he could gather. He managed to cobble together an ad hoc force of seventy-five men. He may, or may not, have known that the Argentine defenders were more than double his number.

The Major had elements of the SBS and SAS (Royal Marine and Army Special forces), the Royal Marines (infantrymen and mortar men) and members of Naval Gunfire Support (NGS) parties (officers and gunners of the Royal Artillery and sailors of the Royal Navy).

The South Georgia Task Force, as a whole, had similar orders to we Interrogators: achieve the aim, but do it in such a way as not to disadvantage Britain's position in any further peace negotiations.

Just before 3pm on the afternoon of 24 April, 1982, exploding shells from the guns of the *Plymouth* and the *Antrim* had 'walked' with perfect precision around the Argentine defensive positions, leaving them in no doubt that they could be blown to pieces if the British wished it. At the same time the land attackers had converged from various directions.

The final decider for the Argentines had been when some SAS men had crossed a minefield to their front unscathed and had raised the Union Jack on their flagpole. Three large white surrender flags appeared soon after this.

The Argentine garrison at Leith, the second largest South Georgia base, had surrendered without a fight the following day, when SAS and Royal Marines had arrived and HMS *Plymouth* and the newly returned regular Royal Navy Antarctic patrol destroyer HMS *Endurance* had sailed into their offshore waters with guns levelled.

The rapid surrender of the man the Argentines had appointed to command on South Georgia was of great assistance to the British Force commander. He was a man internationally known for aggression against the helpless. He was reputedly an Argentine government murderer who was possibly lying low for a bit on South Georgia. It is usual that this type cannot face persons who can fight back. His name was Alfredo Astiz (reports of his rank vary). He reportedly specialized in killing women political prisoners. Apparently he would murder women who had just had babies and then put their children up for adoption among his staff. The French government still wishes to speak to him about the disappearance of some nuns and the Swedish government about the disappearance of some of their female nationals in Argentina.

My team did not speak to him as our commanders thought him unbalanced and felt that nothing of value would be achieved. Sadly, the British government could not find an internationally legal excuse to retain him and hand him over to the countries which were after him. The South Georgia force should have towed him back to Ascension Island on the end of a line. Being food for fish might have been the most worthy thing he had ever done. There does not seem to have been word of any trial by subsequent more democratic and humanitarian Argentine régimes, so possibly they still protect him.

South Georgia was returned to Britain twenty-three days after the Royal Marines' gallant but doomed fight and one month and six days after the Argentine flag was illegally raised on the Island.

The Argentine prisoners-of-war were brought on board the *Tidespring* on 30 April, 1982, and the Sergeant and I must have begun interrogating soon after that. There were 156 Argentine armed forces personnel (navy, marines and special forces) and thirty-eight Argentine civilians. I did not get to meet any of the civilians, so I do not know if they were in direct support of the military or engaged on other activity (survey, nature study, scrap metal collecting or whatever). I believe they were a mixture.

Though there were some injuries on both sides during the British recapture of South Georgia, and not all of these were as a direct result of military action, there were only two casualties. A sailor of the *Santa Fe* was seriously wounded in the leg during the helicopter attack. Royal Navy surgeons had to amputate the leg and he was cared for by British naval medical staff until his repatriation.

The other casualty was as a result of an innocent and understandable, but tragic, misinterpretation that brought profound sadness to all of us on both sides. It was the kind of thing that must have occurred countless times in past conflicts when armed men are keyed up and determined to do their duty.

The British Force Commander wanted the *Santa Fe* moved and rebeached in a different location. He was obviously aware that Captains have been known to scuttle their ships rather than let them fall into enemy hands, so he placed a Royal Marine guard by the key members of the skeleton crew who were to do the moving. The soldiers were told what to look out for and had orders to shoot anyone who attempted to scuttle the submarine. The Argentines additionally relayed their orders in English. There was a moment of ambiguity in the relay. An Argentine Petty Officer innocently reached out for an innocent control panel. A British guard, sincerely believing that he was reaching for a forbidden control, shot him dead.

Also with us on the return journey to Ascension Island were those Britishers who had been on the island from start to finish, but, because of their remoteness, had luckily managed to keep out of it all. They included Cindy Buxton and Annie Price, two naturalist film-maker friends, and a small number of scientists from the British Antarctic Survey (BAS) expedition. Our team had asked the BAS people if they had observed anything noteworthy about the Argentinians. But the main concern of these dedicated specialists was the adverse effect of Argentinians on the environment. They had shot reindeer and wandered among colonies of sea birds and sea mammals. This greatly disturbs the fauna and does the balance of nature no good at all.

When I finally got to meet my little pale pink ellipse friend of the old chart in the gloomy early eighteenth century school hall, I did not see the satanic 'Forbidden Planet' in an icy tempest I had expected;

and as South Georgia can be. It was a sunny and fairly calm day, though there was a breathtakingly cold cut in the air. Grytviken, despite its white weatherboard buildings and tin roofs, had almost exactly the aspect of one of those neat and compact little ports to be found on the Scots outer islands. Its sharply rippled sea twinkled before it and its tan, grey and sombre-green treeless hills rose in tiers behind it. There was a little jetty.

I saw the *Santa Fe*. She had got through a net of encircling British warships and maritime surveillance aircraft, and had reinforced the garrison with forty more marines before she was caught. To assist him to avoid detection, her Captain had left his electronic aids switched off and had navigated the shallow seas with his periscope alone. He was much admired by the Royal Navy. The submarine was a tough and reliable 'Guppy Class' vessel, made in the United States, but now she lay dead in the shallows. Her conning tower was left in the air and showed many wounds — a gaping hole where a missile had entered and myriad tiny holes where machine-gun bullets had hit. She had died on duty and had played her part in history with dash and style.

A final deception was forced upon me before I parted company with the South Georgia POWs, one that I thought it advisable to stick with throughout my time in the main theatre of the war on East Falkland.

The Lieutenant Commander Second-in-Command of the *Santa Fe* was a naval gentleman by any reckoning — courteous, obviously professional, pipe-smoking, unafraid and dignified in defeat. As I appeared to be an affable British official of some sort, he had instinctively reached out his hand and introduced himself. Politely, he had waited for my response. I knew that, as an Intelligence officer, I must not be compromised. However, if I had not made reply, my mask would have started to slip and my effectiveness be at an end; neither did I wish to be offensive. In those few seconds, therefore, I gave the Interrogator that I had become for the duration a name. I used my correct first name, because it was that a fellow officer might unguardedly call to me within the hearing of future POWs, and, in an illogical flash, I took the surname of a politician that I had always thought a particularly hypocritical, self-seeking weasel. As that instantly invented person, I guiltily shook hands.

Less than a year after the war I was kindly invited as one of the representative party from my particular military camp to a little lunchtime reception being held, for some reason or the other, at another camp within the county. There, to my dismay, and incredulity at the astronomical coincidence, I was introduced to a Captain in the Intelligence Corps of exactly my false name.

During a suitable moment in the proceedings, I discreetly drew him to one side and, darting glances over my shoulders, whisperingly confessed to him of what I had done, for good reasons at the time, that stood a remote chance of embarrassing him in the future. I felt it only fair.

Of all British Servicemen who served in that war, I would have been the one most seen, often for prolonged periods, the one most spoken and listened to and, therefore, the one most remembered by Argentinians; and perhaps, once a few pennies subsequently dropped, I am the one most hated.

He was very decent about it all and said that it was unlikely ever to cause him a professional problem and it was quite all right.

I was most grateful and, of course, apologetic and we got on famously. However, as I was leaving, I did think the point worth quietly making that, although the 'Manhattan of South America' was doubtless a good value, magnificent and sun-kissed place for a Northern hemisphere winter break, and I have always loved tango music, he and I should probably give Buenos Aires a miss for a while!

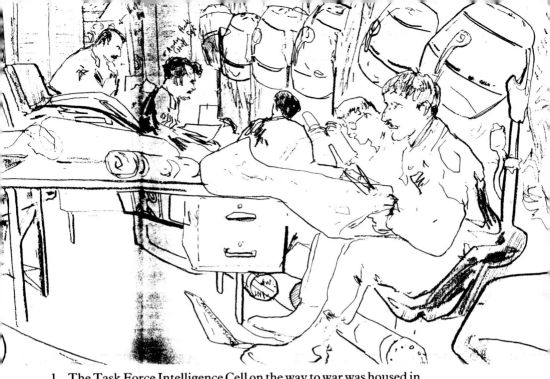

1. The Task Force Intelligence Cell on the way to war was housed in the ladies' hairdressing salon on the *QE2*. This drawing by Linda Kitson, the official artist of the Falklands War, shows the author top left.

2. Port San Carlos just after the first landings — seeming chaos and furious trench-digging for shelter from air raids, in which the troops were helped by the local children.

3. Some of the Task Force ships in San Carlos Water shortly after the landing.

4. An Argentine Mirage of the *Fuerza Airea* attacking Task Force ships in San Carlos Water.

PART III

On to The Falklands

'Hello! What's happening?' Probably the most common greeting between British land combatants during the Falklands Campaign.

Every campaign I have served in seems to have had a particular sound of some sort that, if ever heard again in later life, instantly and vividly resurrects a world and feel of times past. For Vietnam there is the 'whop-whop' of the two-blade Iroquois helicopter; for Kashmir there is the endless chug and smell of the field station generators; for Belfast, it is the night sounds of explosion; shots and alarms; and for the Falklands, for me, it is the above phrase.

The land war on the Falklands became divided. The British Division separated into the two prongs of a pincer movement and the Brigades would divide, at times, into Battalion Groups. The loss of most of the heavy-lift helicopters when the Atlantic Conveyor *was sunk required men to march (or 'yomp' or 'tab') to their particular battles.*

The remoteness of the islands from any English-speaking radio station (except the one in Argentine hands at Port Stanley) meant that almost nothing could be picked up on a personal transistor. This combination of being scattered, slow and independent movement and the lack of reliable radio news bulletins tended to make men feel that they were not aware of the latest overall picture of the war. Verbally, via the orders groups at the various levels, great effort was made to see that every man was kept as well informed as possible. However, the lifestyle of the fighting soldier, combined with the feeling of isolation that the aspect of the islands could induce, tended to retain the sensation of being out of touch with the wider view. One famous Parachute Regiment Battalion Commander and 'character' of the war even had a large notice stating 'Rumour Control' fixed above the entrance to his field bunker!

Conversely, the various headquarters were up to the minute with the general position but were desperate for every snippet of news from the 'coal face'.

Thus, there was an endless chorus of this greeting whenever a new face appeared in any location.

*My constant darting to and fro between the forward troops and the main
headquarters, on any passing helicopter that would give me a lift, either to
inform of important interrogation results or get new instructions, meant that I
heard the phrase more than most.*

*Major General Sir Jeremy Moore, the Commander of the land forces, once
cheerily hailed me with it. This, of course, could have caused one to become
alarmed. However, there was nothing that could worry any of us with such a
Commander. It was merely that the tough, multi-campaigned, valiant and
decorated soldier cared about every one of us and accorded us all, and even
anything that we might have to say, an importance.*

A. San Carlos and Ajax Bay

The scene at Port San Carlos on 1 June, 1982, was as classic and as
epic a composition as British military history has produced. Battalions
of Her Majesty's personal troops were coming ashore and advancing
inland. The big Guardsmen marched in company phalanxes up the
sloping mud track that wound between tussock-covered knolls. A
Scots Guards piper, in an environment identical to his home, played a
brief skirl. It was the sound of a hard and tribal land with a fighting
tradition and every soldier braced up.

Right behind them more men swarmed out into the mud and
pebble beaches, across 'drawbridge' ramps, from their packed landing
craft and quickly shook out into disciplined order and followed on. On
the tops of the nearer low hillocks that surrounded the beachhead were
sentinel teams manning impressive, outward-facing, tripod-mounted
0.5 Browning heavy machine guns.

Great towering sea vessels, grey warships and dulled and mottled
troopships stood in the offshore water. Between them and the small
beach, the white-and-grey camouflaged, motorized-box, landing-craft
(called 'rubbish skips' by the Paras) plied. Helicopters bustled between
the ships or clattered noisily overhead as they hurried inland.

To have really been at one with the giant canvasses of the past, the
troops should, of course, have been in the red tunics of earlier centuries.
However, there was not a question of doubt that we were 'imperial
scarlet' in spirit!

Everyone was dressed in bulky camouflaged smocks that showed
that the quilted 'Mao suit' liner was underneath. The men of the Scots

and Welsh Guards wore khaki berets with bronzed regimental badges. However, gesticulating Staff Officers of Land Force and 5 Brigade Headquarters provided a little colour with the various types of headgear from their Regiments and Corps. There were bright red Military Police berets, the apple green of the Intelligence Corps, the pale blue of the Army Air Corps and a couple of officers displaying the red and white feathered hackle of the Royal Fusiliers.

All men were buckled into uniform dark green canvas webbing with large packs high on their shoulders and the clutch of smaller 'kidney' pouches below it. The advancing soldiers carried their rifles diagonally across their chests. A British soldier, even many miles from a battlefront or on peacetime training, would be reprimanded and possibly punished if he 'slung' his weapon.

I was observing this vast seething magnificence from the top of a beach-bordering, steep-sided mound just off-stage. I was in company with a Guards Captain who, for the moment, had a logistic responsibility, and a Roman Catholic Army Padre. We three had come ashore earlier. The Guards Captain and I had helicoptered in just over a day earlier, slightly ahead of the Gurkhas, and the Padre had landed with the very first elements of the Task Force, 3 Brigade (the Royal Marine Commandos and the Parachute Regiment Battalions), just over a week before. The Guards Captain had been given an early ride to do some advance planning and I had been needed to talk to a recently rounded-up Argentine observation post party.

Three days before there had taken place one of the greatest but most terrible battles that a British, and perhaps any other, battalion-sized force (800/900 men) has ever undergone.

Four hundred or so men of the Second Battalion of the Parachute Regiment, which is the number that forms the fighting tip of a battalion attack, defeated some 1400 Argentines who were in a long-time fortified defensive position with integral artillery and anti-infantry aircraft. The Paras, for various reasons, one being the weather, had very little shell or bomb help.

In non-stop icy wind and freezing rain they made a 20-mile trek from San Carlos over tussock, rock and hill terrain; they had no sleep for three nights; for two days they fought through one enemy strongpoint after another down a several-mile-long neck of land and they hazarded their lives still further to ensure that all the civilian hostages held at Goose Green settlement were liberated unharmed.

Even the most basic Staff College lesson on The Attack will state that attackers must outnumber defenders by a minimum of three to one (six, nine or twelve is even better). The Paras went in without a second thought with the ratio in reverse.

Although their victory was awesome, the price they paid was high. Fifty-three of their number fell. Eighteen were killed, almost all of whom were Officers and NCOs who, of course, led from the front.

As they closed in, it is said that the Paratroopers called jokingly to their Second Lieutenant Platoon Commanders, just out of Sandhurst and just out of their teens, 'You're on, Sir!'

The young men knew that they must perform their ultimate duty.

The brave Commanding Officer went down fatally wounded as he personally charged into enemy machine-gun positions to give his men example and inspiration at a particularly hard point of an unrelievedly awful battle.

Accounts of the number of Argentine dead vary between 150 and 250, depending upon whether one reads British or Argentine reports.

The Roman Catholic Padre had been at that battle. It had been a busy time for him and his Argentine colleagues. He was at our location because battle and bomb casualties, of both sides, needed him in the field hospital at nearby Ajax Bay. There were wounded and dying to be comforted and Last Rites to be given.

On 31 May, 1982, the day that the first major units of 5 Infantry Brigade and General Moore's headquarters came ashore, a Company of 42 Commando, Royal Marines, assisted by SAS, had taken the 1,400ft Mount Kent, the highest and most strategic of the ring of heights that surrounds Port Stanley.

The SAS had been inserted as early as 1 May and had been harassing and 'malleting' (SAS popular jargon for neutralizing by killing or capturing) the Argentine defenders of Mount Kent for some time. General Menendez, the Argentine commander, had withdrawn some of his 12 Battalion from the summit to reinforce Goose Green and subsequently must have felt the peak to be untenable, for, when the British troops stormed on to the top of the mount, the Argentines had melted away.

Despite the freezing damp wind-tunnel of a position that they had to hold, the Marines had looked eastwards with joy; they were the first British troops of the recapture force to look on Port Stanley, the final objective.

They could just see Moody Brook barracks, the extreme western limits of the town, in the far distance. Hard battles were yet to be fought and many more young men, of both nations, would die. However, the British had the enemy's heart in sight and the point of their blade was inching forward. An end to it all might be possible.

As the Land Force headquarters and 5 Brigade's third coming ashore day drew to a close, the first Royal Artillery shells were landing among the Argentine positions close to Port Stanley.

Blue Royal Artillery berets and blue-grey RAF Regiment ones, from a Rapier anti-aircraft Squadron, were now arriving with the reinforcements on the beach at San Carlos. Logistic corpsmen and stores were also appearing, and there, advancing determinedly up the beach was the magnificent and unmistakeable figure of 'Admiral' Hughes.

Major Hughes was not, of course, an Admiral, he was a Forward Air Controller (FAC). This is often a post accorded to distinguished officers of wide service experience, and that 'Admiral' Hughes certainly was. He became known as 'Admiral' because he had for many years been the Army's liaison officer on board the aircraft carrier HMS *Ark Royal*, a job he had loved. Many of his anecdotes began with, 'When I was on *Ark*'.

His active service career had begun in the late 1940s, in Malaya, and had continued through many more campaigns, and now, right at the end of his working life, he had been called yet again. Another FAC and I had shared a cabin with him on the way down. He was a kind, courteous, witty gentleman and a delight to be with.

FACs have more heavy field kit to carry than most (the addition of things like laser range finders etc) so 'Admiral' Hughes had had his golf trolley converted — reinforced, heavier duty wheels, painted in camouflage colours, that sort of thing.

Legend has it that the golf trolley faithfully followed the brave old 'Admiral' for the 70 miles from the beachhead to the outskirts of Port Stanley, via the pitched battles en route. Sadly, it was there struck down by fatal metal-fatigue at the moment of victory. It collapsed and could not go on. It was tittered through the ranks that 'Admiral' Hughes' poor golf trolley went lame under him and he had to shoot it.

Apparently 'Admiral' Hughes officially reached retirement age during the last days of the battles around Port Stanley. We all said that he should get his blazer out of the bottom of his pack, saunter down through Argentine lines, tell them that he was out of it and look for a plane or a ship to somewhere. Obviously he saw his duty through to the end and brought bomb and shell down with deadly accuracy on to enemy positions. In one of the most dramatic sequences of a war film made at the time one can hear 'Admiral' Hughes in voice-over saying things to pilots and gunners like, 'Oh jolly well done, you hit it!'

There are times, I decided, as I looked out on that scene of columns of British troops snaking inland, the sound of the bagpipes and old 'Admiral' Hughes striding up the beach towing a golf trolley, that one starts to have a measure of sympathy for Her Majesty's enemies; for, no matter how outnumbering they may be, against such spirit and style the odds are stacked against them.

The three of us, atop our hillock, heard from a busybodying Staff Office friend who raced past that an Argentine patrol had just shot one of our helicopters down into the sea nearby and their officer had ordered his troops to open fire on our men struggling in the water.

The Guards Captain leaned over me. 'You know,' he said, 'they are not really very *nice* people.' It was as if he were discreetly commenting on 'new' County arrivals who did not ride, kill wild life or keep lots of dogs.

Just as we were about to set off down the steep slope and tag onto the nearest formation, the Roman Catholic Padre raised his right hand above the sea of men. He blessed the soldiers with the sign of the Cross.

'God be with us,' he murmured and inland we marched.

The couple of weeks between the final wind-up of the South Georgia recapture and my arrival on East Falkland had been filled with a bewildering, and ever-accelerating, pile-on of overall war and personal events. The international situation had rolled inexorably into ultimate resolution – mortal combat.

The collective dead and maimed by 30 May, 1982, approached the thousand mark. There were less British casualties as the Argentine's heavy loss events of the *General Belgrano* sinking and the Darwin/Goose Green battle had considerably built up their total.

The British had four warships sunk (HMS *Sheffield*, HMS *Ardent*, HMS *Antelope* and HMS *Coventry*) and the giant stores vessel *Atlantic Conveyor*. About 100 deaths and a large number of wounded had resulted.

Warfare itself had 'progressed'. The age of the 'fire and forget' missile had very successfully dawned. The *Sheffield* and the *Atlantic Conveyor* had both been sunk by a giant wave-skimming, anti-ship missile that, once activated and unleashed, selected a target itself and raced on to it. The two British vessels went to the seabed and a percentage of their crews were burnt to death by a dense fire that tore along the corridors, because, in effect, a huge nail had been driven into their guts, and had then exploded.

All the Argentine Navy pilot had to do was fly his French-supplied Super Etendard long-range fighter-bomber and, when he was still at a safe distance from the British fleet (about 20 miles), release his French-supplied Exocet missile. He could then return to his crew-room or officers' mess and find out what he had hit from the BBC World Service.

Ardent, *Antelope* and *Coventry* had died because they were part of the Royal Navy's line of sentry ships that protected disembarking soldiers.

The bravery and elan of the Argentine pilots who had flown the waves of aircraft that had destroyed these three aroused in the British servicemen at San Carlos, and the listening population in Britain, a scent of their own heritage of a generation earlier. They had a style and a quality not so different to the men of the Battle of Britain.

Five Argentine ships had been sunk so far and two had been seriously damaged. The first to go was the big cruiser *General Belgrano*, with so many young navy conscripts on board, hit by two torpedos. The rest of the Argentine sea casualties were smaller coastguard and merchant vessels that were in fleet support roles. They went to the bottom, or struggled back to port, because of Royal Navy helicopter and Harrier fighter-bomber attack.

Battle action and a few, mostly bad-weather, accidents had caused the loss of about six British Harrier jets and about the same number of helicopters. However, the Argentine aircraft losses by the end of May, 1982, were appalling. Many of the Argentine pilots and aircraft had not been lost in vain, of course – the Royal Navy had suffered near-catastrophic damage, but about a half-century's worth of all categories had been wiped off their inventory. Furthermore, this represented nearly twenty-five percent of their available airpower.

Two Argentine helicopters had been lost as long ago as the South Georgia theatre of the South Atlantic war. A score of their aircraft had been destroyed on the ground by the SAS at Pebble Island and British air-to-ground attack on island airstrips, even before any large British troop landings. 2 Para shot down several Argentine Pucara and an Aeromacci anti-infantry aircraft with hand-held Blowpipe missiles and machine-gun fire at the Darwin/Goose Green battle and, though the bloody confrontation between the Argentine Air Force and the Royal Navy cost the latter three destroyers, it cost Argentina twenty-one aircraft.

The educated and enquiring of the rest of the world, who had initially scoffed at a territorial dispute at the outermost edge of the world that had never been worthy of their study, now aghast and hypnotised, awaited the certain further butchery. Two rich nations with the very latest weapon technology, and operatives well trained to use it, blew apart crafted equipment of astronomical monetary worth and tore, burnt and drowned each other's finest young men.

Just over two weeks earlier I had returned to Ascension Island with the victorious South Georgia Task Force, the Argentine POWs and the rescued British scientists and nature film-makers. Had a profound romance blossomed between one of the younger female civilians and a dashing member of our Force the event would have made a very satisfying, but rather simple, romantic novel or film. The whole saga had been such a tidy tale of British virtue triumphant.

As I had arrived on Ascension by aircraft on the first occasion, I had not had the chance to admire its breathtaking beauty from a sea approach. From afar, the great series of half-haze-hidden peaks seemed to dream on a glittering pale blue equatorial sea. The warmth of the later days, as our ships had gradually inched their way into hotter latitudes, had almost got the Antarctic damp out of the marrow of our bones. How we had smiled at that sun. On Ascension Day, several centuries earlier, the first sailors to behold this precious welcome at the centre of such vastness must have fallen to their knees to give thanks to God.

There was a good spirit in our force, despite some weather-caused frustrations and setbacks that had occurred during the recapture. The force had unquestionably done its duty to the letter and, even if the warships' personnel knew that they would not be going home until the South Atlantic war came to an end, the land servicemen had been given a hint that they would, for practical reasons, be continuing with RFA *Tidespring*. After her repatriation of the POWs duties were over, she would probably be returning to Britain.

The soldiers with the Force were some of the most dedicated members of our Services. Their membership of their élite corps and their selection for the South Georgia force proved it. However, unless one's presence was vital to future events in greater Antarctica, most of us felt, just at that moment, that we could probably have contained our grief should we be passed over for a second session. The Special Forces personnel would, of course, be redeployed to the Falklands.

My trainees were once again at the forefront of my mind. I shuddered to think what my young subordinate officers were doing with them. I also, of course, looked forward with delight to seeing my family again.

However, as I was already only too well aware of the current dearth of Spanish-speakers, I had my suspicions, which was just as well. Before the *Tidespring* had even dropped anchor my Lieutenant Commander had called the Sergeant and myself to him and said, 'Your chopper's on its way. Go and get your kit.'

We had got no more explanation than that, as, indeed, no more was necessary.

Fighting order kit and professional stores could have been a problem for me. As our Intelligence Centre CO was convinced that the Sergeant and I would always operate from an interrogation 'office', with the Aladdin's Cave of our battle box of stores to hand, he had said that we should not clutter aircraft and ship by taking field equipment. This was a most reasonable instruction, as interrogation from a rearward position in comparative comfort is, theoretically, the correct method of procedure.

The character that the war quickly acquired on the ground, of course, meant that the Sergeant and I had to scurry hard on the heels of the most forward elements and we should definitely need our full field kit. Soldiers, of course, become SNCOs because they are the most practical of men; so my Sergeant, despite his respect for our CO, had sneaked his full field order on board regardless. I had hummed and haa-ed for a bit and had finally taken a skeleton order compromise. Thus I was inadequately equipped for what was to come.

However, though I have never had a great reputation as a fighting soldier that I know of, I was once quite admired, even as early as the Indo-China wars, as a most efficient, lucky and discriminating post-battle looter. From the field at Darwin/Goose Green, therefore, I was able, without depriving anyone else, magnificently and fully to complete my field clothing and stores from superb quality Argentine stuff.

My general aspect was as British as one could get, of course. However, I was able to complete my webbing harness with some smart enemy officer-pattern green leather straps and pouches and also found a number of useful little canvas containers that would clip onto my small Vietnamese pack and expand its store-carrying ability. A quick, but thorough, sift through the defeated headquarters produced sufficient stationery for the campaign. I had pens, pencils, rubber and ruler, and even a portable typewriter, which became my pride and joy and which I carried everywhere in its special field case hooked onto my pack, until sadly it was lost in the mud at Fitzroy or Bluff Cove.

The Argentines also produced excellent strongly-bound notebooks and some beautiful writing paper. Unfortunately, of course, it had the Argentine national coat-of-arms at the top. In the interest of correctness, therefore, I used to 'x' it out when writing my reports. However, I did hear that some senior British officers at the Force main HQ, back on HMS *Fearless*, were quite affronted by my notepaper and felt that it was not really 'cricket'.

I picked up a discarded steel helmet so that I had something to wear during air-raids. Obviously, as it was Argentine pattern, I did not wander about our positions in it, for, had I been spotted in silhouette at night, it would unquestionably have been the last thing that I should ever have done.

Just before I went ashore at San Carlos, an untypically friendly and generous Quartermaster thrust a neat little Sterling sub-machine carbine, two magazines and some ammunition into my hands. The weapon was the property of one of our very early wounded who would not carry it again in this war. Thus armed and fully equipped at the eleventh hour, I felt, at that point, that I could go forward and possibly do tremendous things for the British cause!

There had been some days to kill on Ascension until the vast *Queen Elizabeth 2* troopship passed by and my Sergeant and I, and no doubt others, could be helicoptered out and dropped on to it. It would not be stopping. The island was a warm, interesting, busy but friendly place and a brief interlude there before whatever awaited us, which we deliberately put to the back of our minds for the moment, would be far from disagreeable.

Our cups had nearly run over when we were put into a luxury

American-built motel. We were told that as we were the only ex-South Georgia personnel on the island and, indeed, the only ones there who had really been to the ground war so far, and we must have suffered terribly, nothing was too good for us. I was, of course, in total agreement with the prevailing sentiment and, while out of the corner of my mouth whispering to the Sergeant to shut up as he kept saying that the beach with the other soldiers was fine, I graciously accepted the comforts on behalf of us both.

Sadly we were thrown out at about six-thirty on the first morning as some RAF aircrew had just arrived, after inordinately long UK or air-refuelling flights, and it was felt that they were more deserving of the most comfortable resting place available. With one of us vexed and muttering, therefore, the Sergeant and I joined the bivouac lines on the foreshore.

The United States government personnel were as friendly and generous as their nationals always are to people who are open and honest with them. Any British servicemen with spare time, which was very few but did include my Sergeant and myself for a couple of days, were made welcome in the Volcano Club bar, their open-air cinema, shop and canteen. Their attractive wives fluttered a little before the sudden and unexpected influx of military men and caused not a few hearts to beat faster.

I let slip that, on my second tour to the Vietnam War, I had been seconded to the United States Army's Special Forces and a few extra drinks came my way in the bar. It had been a warm, happy and utterly out-of-character few moments during the South Atlantic war.

For a second time the Sergeant and I had the uneasy experience of a dawn helicopering away from Ascension Island and straight out across an empty sea with no solid destination apparent. However, apprehension had vanished at the moment of the breathtaking vision of a colossal, beautiful, streamlined, sea-voyaging city on the light blue plain far below. Gradually we had descended down to it and its vastness grew and rose about us. The moment we touched down duty personnel beckoned our group to dismount instantly, hurry through the double doors they held open for us and enter the palatial interior.

Though the Flagship of the British Merchant Fleet was full of military personnel in working dress and its sumptuous unending acres of fitted carpet were covered by reinforced cardboard to protect it from army boots, it was still totally magnificent. A five-star luxury liner, converted to troopship, provided an unexpected, though very far from disagreeable, way to go to war.

I imagine that the dining-room menu had been trimmed down a bit, but it was still of a variety, quality and sophistication that most of us could never, or rarely, normally have afforded. The QE2 catering staff, like those of the *Canberra* troopship, worked on in their smart livery, exactly as usual, and could not have been kinder or more courteous to us if we had been obese blue-rinsed and bejewelled matrons or cigar-smoking millionaires. Many had witty 'camp' styles of humour and made each meal a delight. They may have been unlikely Britons to have been called to war, but they went and they carried out their duties as diligently as anyone in the force. Above and beyond their terms-of-reference, they made sure that troops en route to a cold and wet campaign, and returning wounded, were given the advantage of top class comfort and care in preparation for their respective ordeals to come.

I had many friends from previous lives on board, including the Commander of 5 Infantry Brigade, and made many more during the week or so of travel from Ascension to Falklands waters. We had long, early-start days of weapon and fitness training, briefings and planning sessions. However, in the evenings, great tri-Service groups of us, in the dining room after dinner or in one of the many lounges, socialized in our unaccustomed splendour. Linda Kitson, the lady war-artist who adapted and related so magnificently to the military, joined my usual group and, besides bringing it some feminine balance, added intellectual and artistic wit.

We threw a cocktail party, that Claridges would have been pushed to rival, within the Falklands Total Exclusion Zone (TEZ), where we could have been torpedoed or missiled, for the birthday of a gorgeous blonde Cunard lady friend of our group.

The first night ashore lying in a damp and dirty shell-scrape, wrapped in a groundsheet while it rained, was, of course, something of a shock to the system after life on the liner. However, hard conditions were the medium we had expected and the initial comfort was just a bonus. I believe, too, that many men were grateful and felt a sense of debt to our war planners for what seemed like evidence of care and perhaps had their already strong feelings of duty and resolve enhanced.

My Sergeant and I quickly organized a double act which I tried to keep racy, and even occasionally funny, in style to ensure that I retained the attention of even the youngest soldier. However, though I used a light vehicle, my message was heavy. In the liner's West End-sized theatre, we took all Units through, and emphasized, the possible life-saving and war-shortening potential of correct POW handling.

We also gave them our impressions of the enemy that they were soon to face. I did not want them to be in awe and deterred in any way, neither did I want them to be contemptuous and over-confident. I wanted to be truthful and try to give them the best picture I could with what little we had to go on. I felt above all that the most important service that we could do our comrades was to remove any positive or negative mystery or mystique there might be in their minds about Argentinian military men; to give the enemy the clearest and most accurate human face that we could.

We recounted the tale of the recapture of South Georgia, which they could not yet know in detail, but warned them that our ground troops too had earlier realized the pointlessness of an heroic stand when naval guns have you in point blank range. The quick Argentine surrenders at Grytviken and Leith might well not be the measure of them.

We took our men through the inventory of weaponry that they would face from small arms to infantry support weapons, to artillery, armoured vehicles and land-based mobile missile launchers. We put up slides of the range of warplanes and described the ways in which the different types might try to kill them. We handed out photocopied sheets showing what the enemy looked like in his field uniform, and the various insignias of rank and specialization. Also on the sheet were a few useful phrases such as:

'*Renda sus armas!*' (surrender!)
'*Manos arriba!*' (hands up!)
'*Ven aqui!*' (come here!)

We got them to shout them out collectively and did an act a bit like the two comedians in the pantomime community singing competition. Everyone roared the phrases out for all they were worth and tried to out-volume the rival half of the theatre. All seemed to find it fun, including, fortunately, the Senior Officers.

I used to be delighted subsequently, when I spotted soldiers rounding a corner, pointing a forefinger at a group of unexpectedly encountered friends and saying, *'Renda! Manos arriba!'* and the others, with mock terror, shooting their arms into the air. I even heard an NCO call to his troops with, 'Oi! You lot! *Ven aqui!'*

Finally, we would give the gatherings our personal impressions and feelings about the Argentines: having access to good training and seeming to know their jobs and equipment well, totally dedicated to the Malvinas Holy Crusade, still confident of finally prevailing, professional in manner and dignified and not overly nervous as POWs.

However, I also presumed to counter this with the reminder that our ancestors had always passed on their tenacity. Our ability to slog and endure and remain unimpressed in the face of foreign displays of might was legendary. If they ferociously implemented their traditional British training they must prevail.

'Anyway, it's an accepted historical basic fact,' I would say as I drew the 'serious' part of the presentation to a close, 'that once the British get among foreigners with bayonets and rifle butts, its all over for the foreigners. I mean, don't we produce the finest yobs in the world?' I would go on to increasing guffaws. 'Our bar-room brawlers are legendary!' I would trumpet in mock Shakespearian actor style and the roar would grow. (I had inadvertently considerably researched this facet of the Anglo-Saxon/Celt, particularly during my student-days part-time dancehall 'bouncer' posts.)

'Our football hooligans are second to none!' I would end in dramatic crescendo and would sweep my classical pose upstretched right arm and vertical forefinger diagonally downwards and across to strike my breast with a fist. I then remained for a moment with a far-away, but inspired, gaze as if I saw the shade of the deity of this noble national quality somewhere in the upper reaches of 'stage left'.

There was little other live entertainment on board for the troops, so I usually got an easily earned ovation. Once the noise died down and just before I asked the most senior officer present if he had any points to add and then to ask his permission to dismiss the troops, I would send them off with: 'By the way, the Int centre is located in the ladies' hairdressing salon, so if we can be of any further help, don't hesitate to come and see us. You can get an Int brief, a coloured rinse and a manicure!'

Just before we all transferred to the *Norland*, or as in my case, the *Canberra*, a little 'gang-show' was organized. By far the most impressive item was the male-voice choir of the Welsh Guards. All ranks stood awed and spellbound in a packed hall as these tall, tough fighting men made the very rafters ring with the powerful perfect tones and lovely harmonies of their race.

I expect that the distress that I saw on the faces of those who pulled burnt and torn Welsh Guardsmen from the sea by Bluff Cove a short while later was made more poignant by knowledge of how cultured these people are, and by the recent memory of their deeply moving music.

I had even briefly called on South Georgia again. Commanders and politicians in London had decided that the Exocet should not be given the inspiration of having the world's biggest sea passenger carrier in its target area and so, in Grytviken Bay, we had all been moved on to other vessels.

The night the *QE2* arrived, I saw South Georgia in strange apparel that I had not seen before, nor could have imagined. I had seen it bright and choppy. I had seen it dark and furious. I did not know that it could be totally still, silent and shrouded. Our giant ship glided into a land of science fiction and 'monster movies'. An endless dome of hushed mist closed about us and bore us away from our world for a while. It rested its gently swirling base about forty feet above the sea, which was as still as a woodland pool.

The smooth glareless surface enabled us to see the marine life of that remote and populous sea. Little penguins, in perfectly synchronized groups, rose and dived past our towering side, large dark shapes wove their way through the depths and great snouts, fins and flukes broke the mirror of the vast twilight millpond.

In the crisp and damp daylight version of the eerie scene, the enormous logistical task of cross-decking the reinforcement brigade and the Force headquarters units, and their equipment, took place; thousands of men, artillery guns, vehicles, tons of ammunition and every possible category of stores (edible, wearable or just generally useful) were hurried across from the *QE2* to the shallower draught *Canberra* or *Norland*.

'I'm afraid it's not going to go very well,' I overheard a senior logistic staff officer say apologetically to a colleague. However, I certainly believe that he wronged himself and his men. Though some units did end up with themselves on one vessel and their equipment on another, the 'logos' worked hard, and without sleep, for over 24 hours and achieved a result that in the circumstances and the time was admirable. The tenders and the helicopters, with underslung loads, were in perpetual motion.

From somewhere beneath *Canberra*'s great flare quietly chugged a little tug on the parting night for the big ships. Her modest and unobtrusive approach belied the significance of her cargo and the effect that she would have on the thousands of warriors who looked down in packed tiers from the dark outline of the troopship. The little tug's deck was covered with men. They all wore one-piece white overalls. Some stood on their own with missing limbs, others needed the support of their companions. The blinded had strong arms round their shoulders and those who could not stand were surrounded by caring groups who held up plastic bottles and tubes and comforted them.

The *Canberra* stood frozen in total silence. Realistic peacetime and intelligent individual reasoning can give novice battlefield soldiers good preparation for war but nothing can ever lessen the shock of when the beast first rears up one of its cruel faces in full graphic view. These men had not been seen before by the new Brigade when they had arrived on board as they had been in the ship's hospital. They were now being moved to the *QE2* and would be going home.

The wounded Royal Navy men who were able to looked up and scanned the row upon row of unmoving faces. They had lost their ships and their friends and perhaps their health forever. They wanted to see a face they knew from another world. They wanted to wave and shout to someone and to smile. They wanted the comfort of the serviceman's familiar daily world of loud exchanges of coarse humour and affectionate derision, but the terrible quiet of thousands of men went on.

In an explosion of grand noise, a military band struck up from the deck of the troopship. To everyone it was a miracle in sound. The relief was intense. The men on the giant ship cheered and cheered and, to the delight of all, the routine exchange of jokes and foul language was soon established. The band played 'Hearts of Oak', 'A Life on the Ocean Wave', 'Sussex by the Sea' and all the marches that would be so familiar to the sailors. Everyone pounded their feet or the rail in front of them and many sang the 'dirty' verses that have been evolved for the tunes by many generations of British servicemen.

When the band ceased, the wounded sang the Royal Navy's and Royal Marine's ever-popular drinking and rugby song, the 'Oggi', in response. There were more deafening cheers from the Army Brigade;

then the little tug became indistinct and shortly vanished as it moved off to where the *QE2* waited in the mist.

These wounded would be the first men who had fought in the war that the British people would see. The display of public emotion when *QE2* arrived at Southampton would be something that had probably not been seen since troop homecomings in 1945.

I did not seem to be long on *Canberra*. Life was almost as luxurious as on *QE2*. There were some terrible seastates during our steaming to the Falklands. At night, as I lay in my bunk, I could feel monstrous water fists furiously pounding and jolting our free-floating world. We had an air-raid warning but nothing transpired.

On my last night aboard a Scots Guards company commander played some lovely tunes of Scotland, I think to himself, on an accordion in one of the bars. He was the courageous officer who personally led the final decisive charge up Tumbledown Hill. He had to shoot, bayonet and club down defenders himself in the mêlée. The Major was a particularly kind and good man.

The Intelligence centre was once again housed in the ladies' hairdressing salon.

A few of my land-service colleagues never got used to the novelty of travelling by ship. 'Avast there below!' I heard one of the two tough, ex-ranker Parachute Regiment Captains, who shared a cabin next door to me, bellow down a companion way just outside my door as everyone was getting ready for the evening meal.

'Send up a new cabin boy!' he roared on in a ghastly exaggerated Robert Newton as Long John Silver voice. 'This one be wore out!'

Great hoots of oafish laughter had then echoed along the corridor.

One of my happiest memories of the *Canberra* is of the enjoyable company of two of the most senior, in years, P & O staff members. They were the cleaning 'ladies' from my corridor. One was indeed a lady. She was almost the archetypal British 'char' lady, kind, motherly, perceptive and raucously good-humoured. The other was an elderly homosexual and had the same manner and fine personal qualities as his partner.

The occasional respite they provided away from warlike preparation was a delight. Invariably I would take morning coffee or afternoon tea with them in their little storeroom cum kitchen. The actual lady wore a traditional country wife's 'pinny' like the mature ladies of my village, but it was in the ship's colours. They too came from the South

Coast. They could have been people that I had known all my life. We chatted lightheartedly of inconsequential things. When it was time for me to go ashore, they were both waiting for me outside our 'tea room'.

Freezing rain was blowing past above decks and I was swathed in the outfit that I had put together last thing before leaving England when doubt about our warm onboard 'Interrogation centre' had suddenly struck.

I had dyed my thick cream polo-neck jersey a dull green in the officers' mess laundry and wore this over my vest, but under my issue khaki jersey, combat jacket and parka. I had bought thermal insoles for my good leather ex-New Zealand high boots. Round my neck was wrapped a long black scarf, that I felt was unlikely to compromise any local camouflaging, and on my head was my corps' blue-grey beret with an officer's badge in bronze. I was loaded with battle webbing and pack and held my newly acquired sub-machine gun.

My friends stuffed handfuls of high class Earl Grey, Darjeeling and China teabags into the pockets of my giant outer smock, as I would have been unable to grasp them with the old-fashioned fleecy-lined flying gauntlets I was wearing. They had procured the special teabags for me from the first-class cabins where the Senior Officers were berthed. It was to give me the chance of a little civilization in the wilderness.

'Well as your mother's not here, I suppose I'd better sort you out!' my lady friend said and pulled my scarf, that was coming adrift, tighter and tucked it in. In age, she was probably not too far from my mother. She also buttoned up a couple of my combat uniform pockets.

I gave her a peck on the cheek and took the homosexual's extended hand with both of mine. He had a slightly theatrical manner and brushed away a tear.

'No, you know me,' I heard him say in the 'tea room' as I walked away down the corridor to the first of several sets of steps that would eventually take me up to the helicopter pad. 'A passenger is just a passenger. You just forget them once they've gone!'

However, they were both out in the corridor again when I looked back from the foot of the steps. We all grinned excitedly at my impending 'moment' and gave a 'thumbs-up'.

*

The first captured Argentines that I had spoken to immediately upon arrival on land did not provide much useful information. However, they were useful to my team and me in a rather negative sort of way. It was not that they did not want to talk, and they had probably not been briefed that they should not, it was just that the Argentine conscript rarely had anything of value to pass on. This was a worthwhile discovery as we would henceforward not waste too much time (and there were only three of us, of course) on those from whom we should not get much of value. Officers, Warrant Officers and SNCOs are, obviously, the most likely possessors of significant military knowledge. However, soldiers can also be, if they are, like ours, encouraged by their military system to take an interest and are kept generally in the picture, to show them that they have worth and to keep their morale up

The Argentine private soldiers, regular or conscripted, were for the most part true peasants and had the peasant's strengths and flaws. In the English-speaking world we sometimes refer to someone as a 'peasant' to insult them, yet we are probably unaware of the critical position a peasant once held in our society, still does in some, and of the character of a peasant. The genus has practically vanished from the North-West European world.

Because the peasant will probably live out his or her life in a hand-to-mouth situation, they have become conditioned not to waste thinking time and energy on thoughts that will not benefit their fine-line existence. In a crudely hutted remote village or outer-edge urban sprawl shanty-town, keeping self and dependents alive and in any comfort available must rarely allow the luxury of being able to enquire, should there be anyone around who knows, what is over the horizon and about current political and fashionable affairs.

British soldiers are constantly inquisitive. They want to know what their unit is doing, and why, how things are going overall and precisely what are the interim and final goals. Most Argentine soldiers seemed not to have asked which companies of their regiment were on their flanks, even if they had been a long time in a defensive position, or made any detailed enquiry of their larger military world.

I do not believe that this was because of any intrinsic shortcoming in their basic make-up, but was a conditioning of both their civilian and military lives. They were civilian peasants who were currently serving as military peasants. They were a layer of their current national systems and passively accepted what was.

However, I had learnt from conversations with British servicemen who served in the Middle East during the First World War, and from books on the subject, that there are problems in coming up against peasant private soldiers, particularly when they are in defence. The lack of inquiry and lack of knowledge means that the peasant soldier is not in possession of facts that should make him fearful. The more aware soldier will realize when his position is untenable and might panic or flee. The simpler soldier may not realize that anything is wrong and may continue to obey his last order (eg: 'stand and fight here') to the letter.

The stoicism of the simple illiterate First War Turks in defence is legendary. Argentine private soldiers also died at their posts when it would have seemed obvious that, so much of their last defence having fallen, their position was hopeless.

The peasant also has an extremely frugal lifestyle. Thus, when a military system keeps him poorly supplied, either through lack of resources or inefficiency, it is likely that, as he never had much anyway, the peasant will keep going while the more sophisticated soldier's morale and efficiency start to flag.

In modern attack or other military manoeuvres requiring all men to know strategic movement and positioning, to have the wit to deal with unexpected turns of events and to have the ability to take an initiative, even a local command, then the thinking soldier is obviously the more effective.

One should not, of course, take personal analogies too far. However, I believe that I got to know our enemy better than most, and their true-peasant rank and file soldiery was a part of the character of their Army that impressed itself upon me. (As did, in total contrast, their incredibly quick-witted and clever-footed officers!)

The group of about five young Argentinians who were the first of the thousands of enemy that the Sergeant and I were to have a greater or lesser discourse with on the Falklands were from a detached platoon of 12 Regiment. Most of their regiment was at Darwin/Goose Green. Two of the group had been shot through the legs when they had tried to escape an SAS ambush. This was, in fact, a very merciful gesture from a category of soldier who is rarely in a position to spend time on non-surrendered enemy. Captain Rod Bell, the remarkable bi-lingual Royal Marines Officer, who played about the most significant behind-the-scenes role of the war, had already spoken briefly to them as he had been present at their capture. We had a bit more time than he had. Not that a more 'in-depth' talk was going to gain a great deal more from the very nice but very young-for-their-years infantrymen.

They were prepared to tell us all about themselves and their unit because they had never been told about concepts like 'interrogation'. However, in keeping with what I came to believe was the trait of their caste, they had not paid much attention. They knew their Section, their Platoon number and almost everyone therein. They also knew to which Company and Regiment they belonged. But there it ended. They argued among themselves over which companies and other units had been on their flanks at Darwin/Goose Green, the names of their officers, where they had been to on the Islands, and when they had been there, and the date that they had arrived in country.

My Sergeant and I could, of course, have been the victims of some clever natural cunning, but I do not think so. However, I was able to give General Moore and Brigadier Tony Wilson, Commander of 5 Infantry Brigade, a reasonable idea of the lifestyle, character, morale and thoughts of the soldiers who obviously made up the majority of those to be faced in the future and how badly the Argentine logistic system supported its troops in outlying areas. I think that these facts were taken into consideration in future planning.

In the light of our experience with the Argentine private soldiers the Sergeant and I spoke to from the Fanning Head ambush, we both independently came to the conclusion that we could, for the most part, eliminate them from our interrogations. After that we usually only used a private soldier to make a quick check that we were still dealing with the same unit, out of a grouped collection or a passing file of POWs, or to confirm a unit's equipment (eg: its type of guns or missiles) or that the names of its officers, that we had previously acquired, were correct.

For weeks the platoon-sized patrol/observation post party had only had a sack of potatoes for rations and each man ate a single bowl of soup each day. When Port Stanley was recaptured the warehouses on the dockside were packed with every type of comestible. Once our aircraft were in action over the islands, one could understand the Argentines' supply problems. However, we discovered that troops had literally been on the bread-line (or potato-line) for weeks before we had arrived or interfered with anything.

A part of our first interviewees' platoon had managed to run from the ambush and they were the Argentinians who made a name for themselves by shooting at downed aircrew in the sea and killing farmers' cattle, mostly for sport or vindictiveness apparently, as they made their way back to Port Stanley. The Sergeant and I got the platoon commander's name and, as each enemy position fell, we tried to find him. However, he had either been spirited back to Argentina or skilfully concealed during our side's at times overly hurried repatriations and, sadly, we did not catch him. The British, of course, wanted to investigate him for possible crimes contrary to the Geneva Convention. His own country awarded him one of their highest gallantry decorations. This was presumably for being the first to report of the British landings at San Carlos and for shooting down two of our helicopters.

'You're to go to San Carlos Settlement and establish an interrogation centre over there,' the Intelligence Corps Staff Captain said. As he was speaking on Intelligence matters, he obviously felt that he should talk down to us in an authoritative and patronizing tone. 'Our Interrogator's already over there. He's already up and running. He will show you where to go.'

'On whose authority is this instruction?' I asked.

'Commander 3 Brigade, of course!' he snapped in reply.

'The Sergeant and I, and *your* interrogation NCO, are a Force asset,' I said.

'Commander 3 Brigade has authority to task you for now,' he said.

'We shall get to the Settlement as quickly as possible,' I replied.

I also extended my hand and introduced the Sergeant and myself. For however long this war lasted, the in-theatre personalities of the Intelligence Corps and my team were going to see quite a lot of each other.

'You'll be choppered to Goose Green as soon as we can organize it,' he called after us as we set off. 'I don't know if you've heard, but it's nearly all over there.'

'I was with a mate who's a Signaller last night,' the Sergeant said. 'We listened in. God, it sounded rough!' He shook his head and looked at the ground. 'They lost a lot you know. And their Sunray went down.' ('Sunray' is the military signaller's term for the commander at any location.)

I acknowledged the Staff Officer's last message with a wave and we dispersed, he to his school hall filled with hi-tech military communications equipment and wall-charts and the Sergeant and I to a little collection of white weatherboard colonial houses and farm buildings on the other side of the small bay.

The Sergeant and I had spoken to the POWs we had hastened ashore to see at opposite ends of a room adjacent to the Captain's borrowed school hall. As we had been winding up, this dapper, aquiline and pursed-lipped Messenger-of-the-Gods had appeared.

I did not inquire how the Sergeant felt, but I was relieved to have my feet, or boots, on firm earth again. Last thing at sea, I had spent some time on HMS *Fearless*, an Assault Ship (a 'mother' ship to the landing craft and a floating dock) and the Force's main headquarters. There had been a couple of air-raids. Rather than be sealed up in a little metal box within a big metal box below the waterline that aircraft were trying to blow up, burn and sink, I used to race to the main deck (I quickly learned the fastest route from any location within the ship) where I had a narrow slot between an external supporting girder and a bulkhead. I was completely out of the way of Royal Navy emergency teams and could stand by to take over if any of the deck-mounted machine-gun detachments had difficulties. I am, or was, an instructor in the use of the General Purpose Machine-gun, and other weapons, in the ground to air role.

I could also, should the order 'Abandon Ship' have been given, have quickly dived over the side. Once in that icy water, I would have died fairly soon from drowning or hypothermia. However, my last sight in this life would have been the familiar sky and not an unfeeling, underwater heavy steel wall that would press me down to suffocating, claustrophobic death in an inky black, nightmare abyss.

The human being, I am now convinced, is a land-dwelling mammal, or most of us are. After the air-raid experiences I did not care if I got shot dead one pace out of the shallows, as I should, with any luck, have had the comparatively better final sensation of my face pressed against my soft damp natural environment for a moment or two.

The Sergeant and I quick-marched and jogged the short, undulating distance between San Carlos port and the settlement. As we closed in we spotted a similarly camouflage-swathed figure, who wore the same blue-grey beret as myself. He had been told of our approach over the radio net and was waiting to meet us. The short, strongly built Flight Sergeant beamed at our approach. He was to be the most competent, loyal and cheerful subordinate, colleague and friend one could ever have had.

He was bi-lingual, quick-witted but patiently determined, and was to be a tower of strength in my tiny unit. In reality he was a Royal Air Force 'boffin'. However, he endured the hardships and dangers of a sub-Antarctic autumn campaign as well as any infantryman. He remained constantly and dynamically operational and eternally cheerful.

Just before our outstretched hands met roars of 'Air-raid Red', followed by 'Air-raid Immediate', reverberated out of the collection of farm buildings to our front. The Flight Sergeant showed us into a dung-encrusted, brick-walled cattle pen and courteously waited for us to choose our preferred parts of the concrete to lie on. He had come ashore with the first Task Force landings and the value of the briefing that he was able to give us on every detail of the entire situation, up to that point, was inestimable.

We never got to know what the Argentine fighter-bombers of that raid did attack. However, to our relief, nothing hit us on that occasion. Once the 'All-clear' or 'Stand-down' was given, the Flight Sergeant showed us, with very justifiable pride, the work that he had been doing.

He had turned the little farmyard that he had been allocated into a well-laid-out 'interrogation centre'. But even before I voiced my fears, he said that he did not think that we should be there for long. Once the Darwin/Goose Green POWs had been dealt with, we should have to hurry after the forward elements. The break-out from the beachhead by 3 Commando Brigade had already started two days earlier.

The main cattle shed he had turned into our administrative and living area and the tea was already made and waiting for us. I thought about the troops advancing inland across that exposed, rain-lashed and windswept territory, and those who were coming ashore to join them even as we stood there, and gave a silent prayer of thanks that in my soldierly old age I had been put out of the elements for a while.

The secluded little covered pens that surrounded the main shed had been cleaned out and allocated variously as holding/waiting bays and interrogation rooms. The Flight Sergeant had even managed to borrow four Royal Marines to assist with our guarding of POWs, administration and area security. The diplomacy that this must have taken, under the circumstances, was awesome. These four tough and extremely pleasant-natured young men stood up to greet me as I entered our 'dormitory'. A totally new type of military role at my great, and less flexible, age had filled me with apprehension. However, my spirits started to rise a little as I listened to the knowledgeable and confident Flight Sergeant. This quality of start to the second stage of my war was beyond my wildest hopes.

Sadly, we did not keep our Marines for long. But, then, we had not expected to. They were of the finest category of infantrymen that our land produces and this precious resource was desperately needed elsewhere within a few days; but by then, and because of them, we were a going concern and, with a bit of occasional ad hoc help, were able to produce Intelligence of the enemy.

The Darwin/Goose Green POWs were to be housed just across a corner of San Carlos Water at Ajax Bay, a quick Gemini boat ride away. The Flight Sergeant had also reserved us an 'office' there too. We could select suitable subjects from the multitudes in the old freezing works chambers, do a bit of preliminary enquiring and probing in our 'office' over there and then take our really valuable cases (officers and technical specialists mainly) away to the more private location at San Carlos Settlement for possible prolonged and concentrated interview.

The system that the Flight Sergeant and I hoped to implement at San Carlos and Ajax Bay did not happen quite as we wished. The goal of some of the senior logisticians who had the administrative control of this first batch of POWs was simply to get rid of them as soon as possible. One or two harassed us regularly: 'Do you really have to mess about with them all this time? I can't see the point of it all. We're moving forward at a good pace anyway. For goodness sake, there's a vessel here just waiting to take them to Montevideo if you will just let us get them on board! We are also combat officers and if enough fall in the forward areas, we shall be urgently needed there.'

I was only a junior officer, but I could have got the back-up of my immediate senior command which, in my case, was Land Force Headquarters itself. However, I should have caused internal dispute on our side at a senior level during active service, and I believe that to be unforgivable. My critics' point about them possibly being called into the field was also a very valid one. I, therefore, tried to meet them half-way.

For the four to five days before we were ordered forward to Fitzroy and Bluff Cove I effectively took up residence in my Ajax Bay 'office' and interrogated virtually non-stop. My SNCOs got back to San Carlos occasionally, as there was little additional, practicable or reasonable space around my 'office' (which was a corner of a POW holding chamber, curtained off with an old piece of canvas). As the Flight Sergeant was such a brilliant Spanish-speaker and Interrogator, I sent him off to San Carlos, when time permitted, with the seemingly better class interrogation subjects.

We selected only the most obviously worthwhile Argentinians. For reasons that seemed of paramount importance at the time, I trimmed my unit's act down to the bare bones and Intelligence information was unquestionably lost. I must take the ultimate blame for this, as I could have made a stand. But the logisticians were greatly helped by having their 'decks' quickly cleared in this area and they undeniably had a myriad of overwhelming problems.

However, the first Argentine POWs were far too quickly repatriated. They arrived home before the war was over. I cannot know all they told their leaders in Argentina on their return or if it was of value to their war effort by then. However, I do know that they described my team and our doings and methods. I realized this when smirking Argentine officers, in the final round-ups, greeted me by my false name, and by then few would give us anything except name, rank and serial number. Notes had probably also been compared with the ex-South Georgia personnel.

I met one Argentine pilot twice. He had been shot down by us on two occasions. The first was in late May over San Carlos Water and the second was just before mid-June over the coast by Port Stanley. He had attacked us and we had sent him home and allowed him to attack us again. He beamed with delight and shook my hand like an old friend at our reunion and asked that his thanks for once more saving him from a watery grave be sent to the appropriate quarters.

The Interrogation unit's problem was not only the unrelenting pressure to hurry up. There was, of course, the other on-going and more serious obstacle to our successful work that I had first realized when meeting the MOD Enquiry team during the South Georgia phase. Few were aware of any difference between military Intelligence-gathering Interrogators and the more pedestrian role of POW 'handlers' (POW administrators, interpreters and guards).

During my first few hours on East Falkland a logistic Royal Marines Major, smiling with relief, thrust a giant package of International Red Cross POW recording forms in Spanish into my arms. He wanted my unique (in that theatre), tiny and overworked team of specialists to be Spanish-speaking clerks. Every POW must be interviewed and his personal details (and, therefore, his existence) recorded.

At this, though it was only caused by ignorance, I did radio the Force HQ for assistance. I did not complain. After two days we got some English-speaking clerks to fill out the forms, assisted by some Argentines who spoke English. I explained to their officers, as was obvious from the forms themselves, that these were not British forms and no Intelligence could, or would, be gathered from them. An Italian priest serving with the Argentine Army eventually took virtual control of this time-consuming business.

Until the British clerks arrived my two SNCOs and I would give the forms a go when we could. There were absolutely no other Spanish-speakers who could be used. The forms were an urgent and mandatory Geneva Convention requirement.

However, by coincidence there was one other Spanish-speaker at Ajax Bay and he was a godsend. He was definitely too valuable to be used on form-filling. He was a bi-lingual Gibraltarian Royal Marines Lance Corporal. His Spanish gave him the essential qualification and he more or less appointed himself the administrative controller of the POWs in the Ajax Bay freezing works. He was a 'character', had a natural flair for the work and was totally accepted, and respected, by all ranks of the Argentines. He had a popular Spanish surname. There was obviously some empathy.

He was outranked many times over in the British establishment at Ajax Bay. However, his respectfully employed effectiveness caused him to be supported and assisted by his superiors.

Several times the Lance Corporal averted potential catastrophe. We were bombed and had regular lighting failures in our windowless and claustrophobic warren of concrete caves. There could have been general panic, riot or attempted mass break-outs. *'Tranquilo! Tranquilo!'* His stentorian roar would fill every chamber and the gathering babble from the packed masses who squatted cross-legged on the cold damp floors would die away and they would sit hushed until normality was restored. Before we all dispersed from the Falklands after the war I sent notes to several members of the command structure in the hope that he might be remembered when the accolades were being handed out.

Half-way through my first day at Ajax Bay I had a sensation that I had not had for many years. During the fairly short period, about my twenty-first year, when I had unwisely taken up an offered university place that I was totally unsuited to at the time, I used to work part-time as a dance hall 'bouncer'. I was hit in the head many times, though never knocked out, and never defeated, I hasten to add. The impact of a blow usually seemed to cause a millisecond of blackness with a bright white starburst at its centre.

'Air-raid Red' was relayed through the freezing works chambers but I cannot remember if it was followed by 'Air-raid Immediate'. The first Darwin/Goose Green POWs were arriving and those of us involved with them had to stay with them. There was nowhere safer to move the POWs to, so we all remained in our outbuilding. The Spanish-speakers explained to the Argentines what was going on and told them to lie on the floor.

We three Interrogators, and our assistants of the moment, crouched in a line facing our prisoners in a large windowless, open-ended barn on the outer edge of the freezing works complex that was part of our POW initial reception area. It was both our British military and Geneva Convention duty to keep an eye on them.

We faintly heard the scream of the jets through the roof, then heard, or felt, the bombs walking towards us. I had heard the deeper and more prolonged roar of bomb explosions before, in the Asian wars I attended, but was far more used to the sound of artillery shells landing and being mortared.

I think that we were more intrigued by the sounds than frightened. The series of explosions had stopped and there was a silence of about five minutes. I thought that the raid must be over. The All-Clear would probably be given shortly. I also considered that we were fairly safe between our two thick side walls. With downward movements of my palms, I indicated to everyone else to stay low while I stood up to get an important captured document that I had been studying from the trestle table to my rear. The moment I got up I got a colossal smack on the front of my body and the blackout and bright white starburst experience in my head.

I was hurled against the table and both it and I seemed weightless for a moment until the concrete floor hit me hard and painfully. I do not remember hearing the enormous noise that the bomb must surely have made. As I grovelled among the fallen bodies and scattered kit I saw that all my team's newly filled tea mugs had been thrown from the table and spilled. For a few moments I was terribly distressed about this.

Then, as the confusion and numbness passed, there came some of the most excruciating pain I have known. A hit from a fist or implement hurts only where it strikes. I had effectively been hit hard simultaneously and evenly all over the front half of my body. A great wall of overpressure from the nearest bomb-burst point had raced along every route of least resistance in microseconds and had smacked every moveable object down as if they had been made of paper.

I thanked God that all those around me seemed to be moving again but their faces were contorted with the blast pain. Mercifully, the external stinging seemed to fade fairly quickly but was replaced by a horrible and unceasing squealing and buzzing type of ringing in the head and bouts of giddiness and nausea.

My companions and I helped each other to our feet just as Medics rushed in from the Field Hospital part of the complex. Despite the fact that our people had been jolted hard, there were no casualties in my immediate area, though some of them looked as if they thought that the end of the world had just come.

It was about the last time that the Fuerza Aerea attacked the San Carlos/Ajax Bay beach-head area. They caused no deaths to our side in that raid and one of their Dagger-Mirage aircraft was destroyed. We later discovered that the pilot, who was killed, was one of those who had helped to sink HMS *Ardent* a few days before.

However, there had been a lethal attack a short while earlier. Four bombs had hit the old freezing works. One had landed on the edge of the complex on the side away from the sea, where the field kitchens were, had exploded and had killed and horribly maimed caterers and troops in the area. Mercifully the raid was not during a meal period when the location would have been packed. Some of the casualties later died from their wounds.

Two other bombs had hit the complex fair and square in the middle. They had passed neatly through our tin roof and had just started to flash through the final few metres of their journey, so that they could bang their detonators on the concrete floor at the centre of the mass of packed bodies and paint the walls with them, when their tail fins snagged between the heavy wooden beams. They jerked to an instant, traumatic halt and now they hung there, reaching down, a tiny distance from their intended goal.

The ATO (Ammunition Technical Officer, Royal Army Ordnance Corps) said that, while the buildings had to be occupied, the bombs were safest left alone. They could have devices in them that would make them go off if he and his team started disarming them. He would sort them out when the building was vacated. The wisdom of these experts in such matters is irrefutable and so we carried on regardless. My office became known locally as the 'bomb room'.

The fourth bomb of the earlier raid was also thought to have gone through our roof but then to have been somehow deflected so that it left by the front door and blew up outside.

That air-raid had killed a number of our troops, despite their rapid defensive deployment drill into their prepared entrenchments, including, I heard, a detachment of the Royal Signals. A bomb landed beside their communications bunker and, although the great earthworks they had laboured hard to put up around themselves protected them from the rip of the shrapnel, the moment of colossal overpressure crushed the life force out of them. They were dead at their posts. There was not a mark on them. They had been instantly switched off.

I just could not believe what had happened to us! I was a very old-fashioned soldier who had fought in limited old-fashioned wars, or at least in the old-fashioned areas of more modern and sophisticated ones. I was used to events where the two sides met up face to face and honestly and personally murdered each other. This distant, technical, push-button and cowardly-seeming stuff I felt was definitely beyond the pale. Though I do realize, of course, that this sort of thing has been going on since 1915, with the first Zeppelin raid on London.

We did not put the International Red Cross sign of 'P de G' (*prisoners de guerre*) on the roofs of the Ajax Bay freezing works as, although prisoners of war were kept there because it was the only local accommodation big enough, the district was a logistic base that was directly supporting a war effort. Thus the display of protective symbols would have been contrary to the Geneva Convention.

Captain Rod Bell dropped in on us once or twice at Ajax Bay and was not very impressed.

5. The author finds time to brush up on his falconry.

6. Sub-Antarctic autumn changed to sub-Antarctic winter during the campaign. The first snow fell as British troops set off for the final assault on Port Stanley, as this photograph of Fitzroy Settlement, taken on 10 June, shows.

7. The official stamp of General Menendez.

MARIO BENJAMIN MENENDEZ
General de Brigada
Gobernador Militar

REPUBLICA ARGENTINA
GOBERNACION MILITAR DEL TERRITORIO DE LAS
ISLAS MALVINAS, GEORGIAS Y SANDWICH DEL SUR

POR RESOLUCION DEL SEÑOR GOBERNADOR DE MALVINAS SE AUTORIZA

AL . . . . ,

portador de la presente, a efectuar el censo domiciliario

ordenado.

El censo debe incluir el llenado de los formularios confec-

cionados a tal fin y emita el documento de identidad transi-

torio.

CARLOS F. BLOOMER REEVE
COMODORO
Secretario General

8. "By resolution of the Governor of the Malvinas Islands, [name], bearer of this document, is entitled to carry out a census in every residence. The census will include the filling out of a special form and the delivery of a transitory identity card."

'The Argentine Officers are well-educated and reasonable men,' he said to me on one occasion, 'and you are keeping them here like animals in pens!' He then swept angrily out.

They live just about as well as we do, I thought, and, with its small regular population, the Falkland Islands just did not have enough buildings in our area to give the 1400 armed and badly behaved illegal immigrants rounded up at Darwin and Goose Green very comfortable accommodation, regardless of their military rank. If anyone knows where the Ajax Bay Hilton is I wish they would let me know, I thought.

However, Rod Bell, besides being an obviously very good and dashing officer of the Royal Marines, a flawless Spanish linguist and an exceptionally clever and innovative man, was a natural gentleman and top class company on the odd occasions when we met up away from the business of the war. He was a Briton who had grown up in Latin America and it would be odd if he did not have an instinctive sympathy for its peoples. He would greet me in Spanish across a multi-Service crowded HMS *Fearless* wardroom. There were senior uneasy glances.

Through some international source I imagine, the British knew, more or less, the Argentine Order of Battle (ie: their inventory of military units) on the Falkland Islands. Thus, one of the most important tasks of my team was quickly to find out, every time we took a position, exactly whom we had met up with. They could then be crossed off the list and our Commanders could see what more they had to deal with. The Argentine garrison at Darwin and Goose Green gave us quite a hard job for a while.

It was not that we could not get people to talk to us. The problem was that there were troops there from no unit or organization that we had expected. We had to identify their origins. It was obviously critical to our Command to know if their Order of Battle list was wrong and, if it was, what was the correct one.

The world's media, including the British, seemed to have announced that a British attack on Darwin/Goose Green was imminent, and it was they, so the British believed, who caused it to be heavily reinforced. Apparently Colonel 'H' Jones, the CO of 2 Para, was in a fury about this during his last hours of life and was pondering if there was any form of legal action he could take against those who caused more of his men to be killed.

Elements of the Argentine Army's 25 and 8 Regiments were the original garrison troops of Darwin/Goose Green and we soon discovered that they had been reinforced by most of 12 Regiment and a battery of 105mm field guns. However, when the POWs were gathered up, there were some 300 extra personnel not belonging to any of these known units. They mostly seemed to be well-equipped and trained regular infantrymen, though the NCOs had blue (air force) insignia on the little tags attached to the left-hand breast pocket button of their padded green combat jackets and not the usual Argentine Army red.

When I demanded to know the title of their unit they all said that they were from the Argentine air force school of airbase defence. This perplexed me. What was a training establishment doing in a war?

I was beginning to learn of the Argentine military's habit of instantly making up ad hoc units from any troops that were available. It is a habit the British avoid, as it is felt that one can end up with 'odds and sods' who neither know each other personally or pro-fessionally, have not worked as one before and, under pressure, fall apart into their original bits. Finally, a fleeting remark made during one interrogation put me on the track and I got the story.

The 'magically' conjured-up 'infantrymen' were the Argentine equivalent of my own Corps – the soldiers of an air force. They were recent classes of students from their corps' training school. When the Argentine command had realized that an attack on Darwin/Goose Green was imminent they did not want to reduce the strength of the force around Port Stanley, so they had sent the air force infantrymen direct from the mainland as reinforcements.

Less than a week before the battle they had been told that they were now rifle platoons and their instructing officers and NCOs were their field commanders. As their instruction involved physical deployment, they had their full fighting equipment with them and had been given a matter of hours to get ready to be flown to 'Las Malvinas'. The training school was at a base with an airstrip, so there would be no time-wasting road travel. They were also senior and well-trained infantrymen because they were on potential NCO preparation, for which only the best are selected.

There was relief among our command that the mystery had been cleared up but also an awareness that the Argentines could be unconventionally innovative. There were a few examples that cost us dear, such as the local modification to the Super Etendard of an extra fuel tank under one wing and its Exocet under the other, also putting the Exocets of the South Georgia damaged corvette (ARA *Guerrico*) into the land defences around Port Stanley. Two of the latter were fired during the last nights of the war. One seriously damaged HMS *Glamorgan*, killing thirteen of her crew and wounding twenty-two.

Though I did have to use more serious methods of interrogation on a very few occasions when the need for some life-saving information was critical, I mostly stuck with the lighter style that I had evolved, after study of the Argentine character, with the South Georgia POWs. There was no time in a fast-moving campaign to behave differently, I considered.

I was the incredibly jolly 'Bertie Wooster' airborne Captain. There was nothing to make anyone fearful, angry or suspicious about me. Why should they not talk to me? I made an amusing break after the trauma of battle and the depressing and uncomfortable life in the POW compounds.

I never lost sight of the direction, and eventual goal, of my joke-sprinkled exchanges. However, I found that, for the most part, I liked, and got on as well with, the Argentine Army and Air Force personnel as I had with their Navy submariners. A young Argentine infantry Major of 12 Regiment also had a Chilean wife. We agreed that the women of that country were the most beautiful in the world, but talk about explosive temperament! It did not bear thinking about. We shook hands sincerely and sympathetically wished each other the best of future matrimonial luck when we parted.

Odd things also happened. As I was interrogating my first ex-Darwin/Goose Green battle POW in the comparative luxury of the first-day-only San Carlos cowshed centre, shouts of 'Air-raid Immediate' once again rang out. I was also the POW guard, so I ordered the Officer outside, with my sub-machine gun obviously at the ready but not, of course, pointing at him. I walked him out of the little compound and indicated my team's air-raid and local defence trench. He and I were the first to arrive at it.

My two companions and I had managed to get the thing dug by taking turns between interrogations, but it still needed the finishing sandbags and camouflage. It was currently just a long rectangular grave-like trough with loose earth spread about it. Nevertheless, it would at least give us some protection. At the sight of it the Argentine

Officer turned instantly towards me. I noticed that he was white-faced but standing to attention. There was a marked upward tilt to his chin.

'*Necesito mi gorra*,' he said defiantly.

'What do you want your cap for at the moment?' I asked in Spanish.

'If I am to die, I shall die as an Argentine Officer, properly dressed,' he replied.

Of course the misinterpretation dawned on me immediately. I did not laugh because I realized how bravely he was behaving in the sincere belief that he was about to be shot and buried in the hole.

'*Non, non*,' I said gently and patted his wincing shoulder, '*Ataque aéreo*.'

The other Britons from round about were hurrying to various trenches in the area that he had not previously noticed, were jumping into them and anxiously scanning the sky.

I helped him down into our trench as he crossed himself several times and murmured the names of saints. As he was something of a military specialist, I do not believe that he had a great deal of new tactical Intelligence that he could have told me. However, after the trench incident he became a very relieved and chatty sort of a chap.

It is probably at least a century since there was as much distance between British officers and their soldiers as there is, or was at the time of the South Atlantic war, between Argentine officers and soldiers. It was not just that the majority of soldiers seemed not overly well-educated peasants and their officers very quick-witted, smooth and smart young Europeans, but the two rank structures were ethnically very different. The Argentine ruling caste is often referred to as Italians who speak Spanish and live like Englishmen. The majority of that part of the population, as evidenced by the 'i'-ending surnames, seem to be of Italian origin.

In the middle of the last century a war was waged against the indigenous Indians that was effectively a war of extermination and Argentina had a fairly pure European population for a while. However, they gradually acquired a new Indian population via illegal immigration from the Brazilian jungle to the north. This seemed to be the strata, with varying degrees of mixed blood, who provided the Argentine rank and file on the Falklands. They almost all came from sub-tropical Argentina – greater Buenos Aires and the town along the northern border. I personally only ever encountered two Argentines (a Petty Officer from the *Santa Fe* and an infantry Major) who lived in colder (Falklands-like) southern latitudes. The hot-climate Army loathed the Falklands weather. I do not remember many mixed-race officers.

The members of the 2nd Battalion of the Parachute Regiment were very displeased with the Argentine officers they encountered at Darwin/Goose Green. Only one of them was forward in the front line of the fight with his men. He was a Captain who courageously dashed about from position to position commanding and encouraging his soldiers, despite being shot through the arm and the leg. He was finally killed when he was shot through one eye.

However, as I got to know the Argentine officer corps, I formed the idea that this situation might have come about for reasons of military or national policy rather than because of cowardice, a selfish self-preservation desire or a lack of concern for their subordinates. A couple of Argentine officers told me that they were instructed to plan and supervise the implementation of any military deployment and, in detail, to explain to the troops the way in which it was to be fought. They were then to withdraw to a more protected location from whence they might have some influence but would not put themselves at risk. The reason for this was that they were an expensively prepared national asset and, therefore, something that must be preserved as much as possible for further use.

One particular way in which Latin-American society usually differs from ours in Britain is that a mandatory part of the apprenticeship for any category of high- or even middle-, ranking public or national office is to have been an officer in your country's armed forces. A British officer, for the duration of his service, can be, and is expected to be, exclusively dedicated to the military world and its every principle, whereas an Argentinian officer is perhaps encouraged to think of the profession as the early rungs of a ladder of ultimately more significant national duty.

In keeping with our original decision, we interrogated officers fairly exclusively; indeed, I believe that we interrogated all officers taken in the early battles (Darwin/Goose Green and Top Malo). We also spoke to a number of Argentine Warrant Officers and SNCOs. However, they were less forthcoming than the officers. This may have been because of trained and disciplined reserve before officers (myself) and authority figures (the other Interrogators) rather than because of a determination to resist interrogation. The officers, although wary, would speak with us if matters were kept uninterrogation-like, and facts or leads would surface.

Until very late in the war, when accounts of my unit got back to Argentina, it seemed as if the Argentine military had not given its troops much, if any, formal training on being a POW and the relevant aspects on the subject from the Geneva Convention. However, in fairness to Argentina, I do not remember it featuring as a universal or mandatory subject in British basic military training either. I believe that it should, for ignorance of it can, at the least, lose for your cause elements of surprise and tactical advantage and, at worst, result in a catastrophic revelation of every detail of a war effort.

This pre-war study is not, of course, likely to be a favourite with either commanders or troops because it admits to the possibility of local or general defeat at a time when the forging of a determination-to-win attitude and high morale are paramount.

From the Darwin/Goose Green POWs, and a few other groups of early captives, my team confirmed the Argentine Order of Battle, established fairly well the strengths, and in some cases the names of the defending units, of the enemy positions around Port Stanley, found some definite and some probable minefields in the path of our advances, built up a much fuller picture of Argentine Falklands defence policy and methods of deployment and established a good overall picture of their morale, general condition and feelings.

Not everything was gained from interrogation. A great deal of our information came from translating captured documents: military orders and lists, instructional manuals and individuals' personal diaries. This was an especially time-consuming and wearysome task in the windowless and poorly-lit Ajax Bay complex.

However, there were brighter moments in the mental and verbal slog, the squinting at screwed-up, muddy and sometimes blood-soaked bits of paper and the near sleeplessness. Every category of high-ranking British military person, including all our commanders, would regularly take helicopter or small boat rides to drop in on us. They all, of course, wanted to know 'What's happening,' and anything new and interesting that we had found out. Without exception they were some of the most considerate and courteous men I have met. We of the Task Force were very lucky. All the vain and uncomprehending who worm into high ranks in peacetime had been left behind.

A particularly cheering occasional caller was Lieutenant-Colonel

Michael Rose SAS. Twelve years after the Falklands war, as Lieutenant-General Sir Michael Rose, he was to take the unenviable command of the UN forces in the anarchic former Yugoslavia.

However, in general, although I hoped that my unit was being useful, I could not wait to see the back of Ajax Bay. Action was obviously imminent further across East Falkland and it was there that I believed we should be. I did not think that there was much more that inglorious deception could get from the POWs held in the old freezing works. The place was a sea of wet mud and grime, the ever damp sky always seemed to be a slate grey, the logisticians and I had unavoidable conflicts and our dead companions were in a horrible great bog-water-filled open pit out at the back.

I did not, of course, imagine that the Falklands climate might be better in any other part but I yearned once again to be the open-air forward-moving British foot soldier that I had been when I was very young.

My inland move with 5 Infantry Brigade on my second day ashore had turned out to be a damp squib. The initial plan had been that the Flight Sergeant and Sergeant were going to stay and sort things out at San Carlos and Ajax Bay and I, the Officer Interrogator, would be the mobile 'specialist' in the front line. However, after I had 'yomped' or 'tabbed' (RM and Para expressions respectively) about ten miles, word came via the radio that I was to walk back to the beachhead as the work-load needed everyone who was qualified. I suspect that the eagerness to be rid of the mass of inconvenient and unproductive foreign bodies also played a part in making my country ramble brief!

When I occasionally got out of the cavernous POW warren of chambers and into the daylight I had a couple of memorable encounters with the local natural life. There was a penguin, who lived on Ajax Bay beach, who was absolutely thrilled by our arrival. He would tear excitedly from one working group to another to see what they were doing. He kept climbing into empty cardboard boxes because they were new and interesting things to him. Soldiers were forever gently lifting him out and putting him back on the ground because they needed the boxes. If there was a discussion going on by the beach, he would race up to it, his little head pushed forward, his arm-like flippers stuck out and his feet twinkling. Upon joining the group, he would look in fascination from one to the other as they spoke. I saw chaps, often senior people, get quite disconcerted by this scrutiny, and conferences dry up and disperse, leaving the bird bewildered until he spotted another novel outbreak of human activity in his area and off he would go again.

A sea leopard erupted from the water right alongside a little Gemini boat as I was stepping from some rocks into it to go across to San Carlos. It was a hefty, twelve-foot-long, predatory sea mammal. Its giant, smooth dog-like head had a mouth that displayed huge canine teeth and there were faint leopard spots on its flat and glistening short pale fur. The Royal Marine coxswain and I, with difficulty, prevented each other from flying backwards over the opposite side of the boat with shock. It was a classic 'monster movie' sequence. We sat hypnotized and paralysed while it dived several times and reappeared, towering above us, at different points along the side. For the moment we were not capable of scrambling back out of the boat.

Though our fear did not greatly abate, it soon seemed that this creature too was intrigued and not aggressive. In fact the expression on its face, as it leaned forward to study us more closely, gave the impression that it would not have minded having its head stroked. However, although I have never heard of a human being eaten by a sea leopard, this one certainly looked as if he could have made a good attempt and he could definitely have removed an overly familiar hand. I therefore sat still, with the most unprovocative expression that I could conjure up on my face, until he lost interest and vanished to the depths. The coxswain did the same.

The front part, that is to say the side nearest to the sea, of the old freezing works complex, which contained the holding areas for the first Argentine POWs of the war, was Royal Navy Surgeon Commander Rick Jolly's Field Hospital. This innovative, industrious, brave and skilled medical man was one of the towers of strength of the war. His men, from all Services, were of a like quality. Nothing could deter him from producing standards of medical care for our forces, and the wounded Argentinians, that in the circumstances were astounding.

He planned and supervised the quick conversion of commandeered merchant ships into top quality hospitals. He welded his vast variety of medical personnel into the most efficient team and prepared them for battle casualties. He also ensured that the already first-aid and self-aid-conscious British infantry were kept supplied and up-to-the-minute with the latest developments of the 'oppo' or 'buddy' system (ie: every soldier is covered, in the event of wounds, by a nominated comrade).

The Surgeon Commander had his helicopter flown into Argentine infantry ground-to-air machine-gun fire to try and save downed Army Air Corps pilots. He and his men were several times bombed and strafed and medical personnel were killed. However, nothing could have stopped the constant care for the casualties of both sides for a moment.

Because Paras and Marines were the first British customers at his Field Hospital, Surgeon Commander Jolly had the sign 'The Red & Green Life Machine' put above the main entrance. The title was a tribute to the respective wine-red and dark green berets of the soldiers. Throughout the war the 'Red & Green Life Machine' received about thirty casualties a day, many of them horribly wounded. Almost all of those who arrived still alive at the Field Hospital lived. When the medics first got to the freezing works there were sheep and their droppings in there. It was cleaned out and established within hours, in time for the first wounded.

I was hurrying to the main doorway of the freezing works complex one day clutching my team's tea mugs, as I had heard tell that there was a tea urn operating somewhere. As I was passing the Field Hospital's tarpaulin-covered front entrance, just to the right of the main doorway, a Medic came out. Obviously guessing my mission, he said, 'We keep an urn constantly going just through here. No one will mind your lot filling up whenever you want to.'

Expressing my gratitude, I followed him as he went back round the tarpaulin and was quite overwhelmed by the pile of thick oatmeal biscuits that he put into my hands for my chaps. He, of course, had to hurry off, so I filled the mugs at the urn and then turned and saw the furiously busy canvas-lined chamber in detail.

There was a bench along the wall just in front of me where the walking wounded sat and waited. The nearest to me was one of those older Junior NCOs who end up working in the stores. They are the 'salt of the earth', but have reached their ceiling because they are not overly bright. Something had blinded him in the left eye. There was a wad of blooded field dressing in the eye socket. He still wore his several-times-repaired, old-fashioned Forces-issue glasses with the left lens smashed where the bomb splinter, or whatever, had gone through it into his eye. He was dumpy and middle-aged and his Royal Marine beret was very old. He seemed to find comfort in a tiny end of a soggy-gone-out, roll-up that he occasionally put to his mouth. He was obviously in shock and made unending clichéd small talk to me about the weather and other irrelevant things. I wanted to put an arm round him and try to comfort him. However, that would, of course, have been incorrect.

I looked up from him and on a nearby operating table was a young Briton who was being held in a sitting position by two Medics while a Doctor appeared to be trying to get a bullet out of a lung. He seemed to be conscious as his face was contorted in the most terrible pain, but he did not cry out.

Every time overworked Medics hurried past a young Argentine Indian boy, who lay motionless on the waiting bed nearest to me, they would quickly put a hand on his neck pulse. After a couple had done this, a third stayed a while longer, feeling, then looked at those nearest to him and shook his head. He called some orderlies who put the dead body on the concrete floor for a moment while they replaced him with a pale and silent Paratrooper whose chest was a mass of red bandage.

Medics or orderlies kept putting more and more huge brown paper bags by the doorway. It suddenly dawned on me that these contained the lost limbs of the amputees and other human parts that could not be saved; I could not stay there any longer.

I hurried back to my area, distributed the tea and biscuits to my men and then went in to the near total dark at the back of my poorly lit office.

In five different places I have had to see things like this, I lamented; most 'military' men don't even have to see them once. I'm forty now. It's not fair. Any number of other, unrelated and not very relevant sadnesses were probably resurrected by the feelings triggered by the sight of the wounded.

I might have wasted more valuable time on self-pity when I should have been doing my wartime job had not the Flight Sergeant burst excitedly in after a few moments. He had uncovered some very important 'hard' Intelligence. Mercifully, the near pitch black that I was standing in meant that he could not see me clearly, so while he was enthusiastically trying to read his notes, I was able to wipe my eyes on the dirty sleeve of my combat uniform.

I was bitterly ashamed. Others had been involved in this war far more intensely than I, and here was the Flight Sergeant, the best member of the unit, who had been on shore longer than I and had been through all the worst air-raids, both on board ship and on land, still keenly, and without thought for himself, getting on with the work.

About four days after my unit started work at Ajax Bay I was told to get my two subordinates up with the forward elements. The Flight Sergeant was to go east to Teal Inlet and join 3 Commando Brigade and the Sergeant south-east to Fitzroy where 5 Infantry Brigade were getting established. I was saddened both by the loss of my friends, and two-thirds of my 'unit', and by the fact that I had to remain at Ajax Bay, now that I considered that most Intelligence had been gained from the POWs there.

However, I was told that a Spanish-speaking officer would be very useful to help manage the imminent repatriation of the Argentines and that was why I had been kept back.

The next instruction that I received did not impress me either. It had been decided that Ajax Bay would remain the POW centre for the entire war. The Port Stanley and other POWs would be transported there when captured. I was to work at either improving the existing POW facilities or establish new and better ones. My two SNCOs would be returned to me at Ajax Bay eventually.

Anything was better than the lightless and foul-air inner chambers of the old freezing works, I decided. Logistic Marines kept washing it out with stringent and asphyxiating disinfectant. The cleaner, whose intentions were obviously of the noblest, would then depart to his own area leaving us coughing and spluttering with streaming eyes and noses.

There were quite a few old offices and other buildings in the area and, as I studied them from a slight distance, I decided that by using them, I could organize a far more efficient and better work environment. However, as I entered each one, I found that members of our force, who could not be bothered to walk to the established field latrines had defecated in every one. I had no work party or sufficient personal time to begin the loathsome business of cleaning them out, so I started to draw tentage.

I was at a low ebb when I was given the good news of a change of policy. Future POWs would not be sent to Ajax Bay and I was to get myself forward to Fitzroy where my subordinates awaited me.

*

I returned to the Falklands about eighteen months after the war was over. Whoever thought out postings would still not acknowledge that I had done anything of a commissioned military nature during the two decades before I enlisted in the RAF Regiment in 1980, so I was given the most junior officer post in a garrison duty unit.

I took over from a very young man who had been one of my students on a basic officer course that I had run just before the South Atlantic war. It was about the most boring and unsatisfying period of my life. Mercifully, I managed to escape from it within a year, albeit under prejudice for notifying the authority responsible that the posting was an error.

I had a happy reunion with the San Carlos farmer, and his young son, whose cowsheds I had briefly used for interrogation and accommodation and I stayed for a couple of days in a new British Army camp that has been built nearby. My first defensive trench was immediately above the small, quiet and dignified military cemetery at San Carlos. I once fired my machine gun across where my companions now lie.

One morning I put on my running kit and jogged the coastal miles round to Ajax Bay. I had a reticence, and almost a phobia, about seeing the place again, but I knew that I had to go. Little of the fighting drama of the war had happened there but much of its sadness had.

When I finally breasted a hilltop and saw it again there was a quickening of the pulse, but only for a moment or two. It looked so different. San Carlos Water was empty of warships and supply vessels, indeed all vessels. The grey complex of large hangar-like sheds and their surrounding buildings looked quiet, tidy and deserted. The mess and bustle of the war was long gone.

It was a blustery but sunny Falklands day. The clear blue sea was flecked with sparkles, the pale corn-coloured hills looked warm, the blue sky went on for ever, the air was so fresh it thrilled and, far below, the Ajax Bay complex looked contented.

I ran and jumped my way down to it. I wandered about and tried to remember what had happened there and to visualize the faces of my friends. I went to the raised area behind the big sheds where our early dead of the war were first gathered and then initially buried. A large symmetrical rock with a neat brass plate on it now marks the place. There could not be a simpler monument, but I think it is very dignified and I doubt that the very straightforward men that it commemorates would want anything different.

I attended that burial ceremony. It was a damp day and some of the bravest men ever to leave our shores wept there. As the Padres intoned the final words the soldiers cast handfuls of Falklands earth, the stuff for which their friends had died, down into the sodden communal grave and splashes of water rose up and fell back.

Excessive demonstration is not, of course, for Englishmen, but I thought for a while, said a prayer and gave their rock a hug.

Inside the chambers I met members of my original Regiment, the Royal Artillery. A Rapier fire unit was deployed nearby and its detachment was housed in the buildings, as Argentina, petulantly, would still not declare an end to hostilities. The Sergeant who commanded them was a fine and cheerful man and kindly invited me to lunch. The Gunners showed me the excellent work that they had done to make the place more agreeable. All the great chambers were beautifully clean and whitewashed and organized into their common room, dining room, offices, stores and dormitories.

The place had once been, or had seemed, filthy because the war would not allow it to be otherwise. Sickeningly messy wounded and dead had been constantly hurried along its corridors. There I had, with a smile, convinced or coerced frightened and miserable prisoners to tell things that they should not have done. The threat of air-raids had meant that we had lived in constant unease. The desperation to give the very best support to the front line troops, and the ceaseless hard work, had often caused tempers to be short. The scream of jets, the blow of explosion, the roar of departing warship missiles and the cacophony of gunfire had shaken the nerves.

However, the place had such a different aspect after the war, thanks to the Sergeant and his men, that I even forgot to try and work out what had been the former use of the room in which I ate my wholesome, army tinned ration lunch, which was probably just as well. The only true indoor reminder of the war was a fine epic poem by a member of the Scots Guards that, in impressive sign-writing, covered one wall. It was, not surprisingly, entitled 'Tumbledown'.

When I got back to the brow of the headland above Ajax Bay I took a quick look back. It was illogical that a critically useful place at the time, which had provided essential war-supporting functions of many kinds, should have taken on such a gloomy, almost satanic, aspect to me and others that I knew of.

All pretty places seem to be smiling on a sunny day, so I smiled back at Ajax Bay and then jogged down the back of the headland and we went out of each other's sight. We were at peace together.

Fitzroy and Bluff Cove

The land about the Falklands sheep station settlement at Fitzroy just before dusk on 7 June, 1982, was as full of British military personnel, warlike equipment and bustle as frenzied as any I had so far encountered since the campaign had begun.

The area called Fitzroy straddles a headland that juts out eastward into the South Atlantic. Bluff Cove is a small neighbouring natural harbour, a matter of some hundreds of metres of water away on Fitzroy's landward side. The two places are connected by a narrow bridge-type wooden walkway. Fitzroy is where most of the local population seem to live; indeed there are some very attractive two-storey colonial houses there, though there are also dwellings and working buildings across at Bluff Cove.

The second the little Army Air Corps Gazelle helicopter that had given a couple of 5 Infantry Brigade Staff officers and myself a ride from Ajax Bay touched the ground we raced out of it, ducking under the blades and dragging our packs after us. Every helicopter that 5 Brigade could get hold of, regardless of size, was desperately needed to get the area fully defended and provisioned so that it might be the firm base for the Brigade's impending curving thrust up into the south-western area of greater Port Stanley. Our helicopter could not get back to the beachhead or Goose Green fast enough.

3 Commando Brigade was established on, and forward of, Mount Estancia about twelve kilometres due north of Fitzroy and its units were concurrently girding themselves for their synchronized sweep down from the north-west towards Port Stanley. Many men were still to die and some bitter, localized hand-to-hand battles were still to be fought, but the intended British 'ring of steel' was closing around the enemy. Although the Argentine commanders, both on the Falklands and in Buenos Aires, must have reasoned that the writing was on the wall for their invasion, most of their middle and junior ranking officers

and their soldiers, because of disinformation, ignorance or childlike Latin vanity, still thought that all was going reasonably well for them.

Every nearby hillside was speckled with moving British infantrymen. They furiously dug trenches, cleaned and maintained their weapons and equipment and, here and there, one brewed up a warm drink for his hard-working friends. Alongside the Fitzroy settlement, at the centre of the area, was the logisticians' stores reception point and men swarmed about with the eager and devoted busyness of termites. Helicopters had dumped great square underslung loads and other items had come ashore from ships. The functional-looking but not unstately landing ship RFA *Sir Tristram* sat in the harbour. The job of the logistic workers was to get the critical equipment dispersed and camouflaged or under cover before the attention of the Fuerza Aerea was drawn to the district.

Falkland Islands men from Fitzroy and Bluff Cove, and their children, were everywhere working with the army storemen. They moved loads with their tractors and trailers, loaned their other vehicles and gave of everything they had. The dour ruddy-faced men of a harsh and frugal land seemed to have a fierce gleam in their eyes. Foreigners of alien blood, language and life had violated and humiliated their home, but the day of reckoning had almost come!

The maroon berets of 2 Battalion of the Parachute Regiment were in evidence round Fitzroy and the khaki berets of the Scots Guards were on the forward and mainland side at Bluff Cove. The big Household soldiers were working hard and well and looked impressive. However, the victors of Darwin/Goose Green, though superficially they had the same outward aspect of any other young, fit and campaign-muddied British soldier, had an indescribable air about them. There was unaffected style, dash and panache, and a single unbreakable spirit of awesome power among them for every military unit to envy.

Brigadier Tony Wilson, the Commander of 5 Infantry Brigade, had done a tactically and morally courageous thing. Upon his arrival in theatre, Major-General Sir Jeremy Moore had told him to get his Brigade to Fitzroy and Bluff Cove as soon as possible so that his units could be in readiness for the attacks on the fortified Argentine-held hills that ringed the landward side of Port Stanley.

The weather had become even wetter and foot, tractor and tracked vehicle movement even more difficult and slower, and it looked as if his advance would be a prolonged affair. The portion of the attacks allocated to 3 Commando Brigade, that had come ashore over a week before 5 Brigade and whose units were more or less in position, might be held up by his command. However, a senior member of the newly liberated community at Goose Green mentioned that, although the Argentinians had cut all the Darwin and Goose Green civil telephone lines, Swan Inlet, about 20 miles in the Fitzroy direction, might still have communications.

A patrol from 2 Para (who else!) flew in armed helicopters to Swan Inlet, on 2 June, 1982, and a Colour Sergeant found a working telephone in a shepherd's hut. He cranked the handle twice (the indicator for Fitzroy) and spoke to a teenage girl from the settlement. She fetched her father and it was established that the place was not garrisoned by Argentinians. Brigadier Wilson, therefore, decided on a bold and fast move by helicopter and ship.

He got 2 Para, recently assigned to his command, in immediately to secure the position, using every helicopter he could commandeer, and the Scots Guards were sent by assault ship over the next few days to back them up. The Brigade headquarters and supporting troops and stores arrived fairly soon after and on 8 June, 1982, still more of his infantry arrived. Much of a battalion of the Welsh Guards steamed into the harbour on board the landing ship RFA *Sir Galahad*.

His action was not without risk. He bent some rules and apparently some of the Force's senior planners made tight sphincters of their lips and sagely shook their heads. However, for the thousands of us who did not have to spend several victory-delaying days on an avoidable, soaking and miserable slog over ever-deteriorating miles of peat bog, he is a fine and dashing commander.

Brigadier Tony Wilson had a deceptively laid-back manner, yet he was one of the foremost soldiers in the South Atlantic war. He held the Military Cross and had previously been in action in Cyprus, Malaya, Borneo, Aden and Northern Ireland. When a scapegoat for a disastrous air-raid that befell us at Bluff Cove was being sought by those at distant and senior levels, I heard that attempts were made to blame the Brigade Commander. We, who were there, know that what occurred on that day was not remotely related to a most original, inspired and sound tactical decision.

As the helicopter clattered up off the ground and whirred away into the hills, I ran into the centre of the logistic activity and asked someone where the Interrogators were. A group of blank looks surrounded me.

'The ghooley-tweakers? The Nazis?' I offered and comprehension broke out everywhere.

'In the sheep-sheds,' several said and fingers pointed out the wooden complex nearby.

Had the British forces not brought us up very carefully, I could have flung my arms round the shoulders of the Flight Sergeant and the Sergeant when I saw them. They also seemed reasonably happy to see me; at the least I represented a 30% increase in unit strength. They had both had adventures of various sorts in the different areas of the conflict in which they had spent the last few days – patrol action, small contacts and fire fights mostly – and they recounted them to me.

There had been no major battles for nearly a week but about a dozen green-clad, grubby Argentines squatted on the dirty floor of a fenced metal segregating pen. Fighting patrols out dominating the area towards Stanley had gathered them up.

The rest of the main shed was being used by the infantry, in rotation, to gain a little occasional shelter out of the freezing wind and drizzle. Within a few days we would fill every pen and bay in the complex with various categories of prisoners; our forces would start to roll forward again and the outer battles for Port Stanley would start.

Once again the courteous and clever Flight Sergeant had secured us working and living space that, under the Spartan circumstances, was of above average quality. The pens in the sheep sheds would allow us to organize the POWs into clearly defined groups: those to be interrogated, those that had been interrogated, officers, NCOs, techni-cal specialists, soldiers and any other divisions or sub-divisions that we deemed useful.

For our personal living space the Flight Sergeant had found an empty cubicle-bedroom in an outbuilding. Our sleeping bags and packs would just fit on the floor. It was damp, cold and unheated but luxury compared to the domestic circumstances that we had known since we had come ashore. We also, of course, knew that the majority of the land force had to live, and keep constant watch, on sub-Antarctic hillsides. The last person to occupy the room had been a fan of an English football team; posters of players covered the walls. In the event, none of my unit got more than the odd couple of hours cat-nap in the room during the three or four days that we were there.

The Falklands weather was deteriorating from bad to worse and, as the autumn started to turn to winter, the gales blew stinging sleet into our faces instead of stinging rain. However, even though the vast concrete hangars at Ajax Bay had given greater protection from the elements, we were all cheered to be at Fitzroy. There was a feeling of being bogged down at Ajax Bay; here we felt that we were on our way again and our spirits soared.

A Falkland Islander Royal Marine had arrived at Fitzroy with our advance party and had liberated his own wife and baby daughter. His friends would call at his in-laws' farm to take turns at nursing the delighted little girl.

One youngish and tough-looking local farmer told me of the Argentinians' regular visits to the settlement. Their behaviour was bad. They delighted in threatening them with their weapons in the hope of achieving a cowering and servile response; apparently they were disappointed. He said that one day a helicopter arrived that already had some men from Port Stanley in it. He and a few other Fitzroy and Bluff Cove men who were in the habit of answering the Argentines back were put on it. The aircraft flew to a remote and uninhabited area and the civilians were ordered out and lined up. The Argentine soldiers lined up opposite them and had their weapons at the ready. The farmer was convinced that their murder had been officially decided upon. It was, after all, common practice in Argentina.

The officer in charge seemed to be getting events finally organized when the pilot, who had remained in the helicopter, called out that he was wanted on the radio. The islanders, who understood Spanish, could not hear clearly what was being said but an order was obviously being rescinded, and it did not please the officer. He protested quite heatedly for a while. Finally, and in an obvious fury, he ordered all the men back on to the helicopter and they were roughly pushed out at their original locations.

Locals were not the only civilians around. There were journalists, photographers and film makers. They were obviously aware that future action, and good news stories, were about to start. They were billeted in one of the main farmhouses with the senior officers. A few regularly disputed military orders that inconvenienced them – things like the requirement for a 'blackout' as soon as it got dark to keep the Argentine night-flying Canberra bombers off the settlement.

A very witty Royal Marine was running the seniors' dining room in a large farm kitchen. On one wall was a big menu chart. Every possible Cordon Bleu dish was listed on it. However, each one had been crossed out and the word 'off' written beside it. The only thing not 'off' was the last item entitled 'compo stew' and, indeed, that was what we always got. Nonetheless, he and his assistants ensured that it was as well prepared as possible under the circumstances and he produced as many 'extras' as he could (Army biscuits, a tin of cheese and some local fresh potatoes and carrots); but, best of all was his humour, flair and style. He cheered worried and tired officers and made no small contribution to victory.

For much of my first night at Fitzroy settlement, and for most of the nights I was there, I joined a Ministry of Defence civilian electronic intercept expert, who had set up a magnificent technical equipment cell in a tiny hut, and listened to Spanish-speaking voices that he found in the air waves.

I think that we discovered an Argentine Hercules transport aircraft, probably creeping into Stanley airfield, on the first night. The pilot was very sparingly, and at great intervals, saying code words that probably indicated his progress to the Fuerza Airea Air Traffic Controllers at the airfield. The background roar of aircraft engines was very familiar. We reported our suspicions so that our Harriers might take a look if it was desired.

An Argentine Hercules was shot down by a Sea Harrier during the war. I have travelled in them in every war that I have attended, a period that spans twenty years. I know that I should not, but I find that I do so hope that that Hercules was not packed with troops, as all those that I had travelled in were. We would all be crammed together on the excruciating canvas and metal seats, passing each other magazines, paperbacks, bits of chocolate and biscuits. There was always a bit of excitement, a feeling of adventure, some apprehension about the destination, and a thankfulness that you had friends together with you.

The thought of one of those great containers, spinning, with screaming gaps in its fuselage, fire sweeping its length and the last minutes of life of its smashed-about pack of familiar humanity, is not one that I can bear to contemplate. I quite hope that I did not have an indirect hand in such an event.

Not long after my arrival I was summoned by Brigadier Wilson. He urgently wanted me to find out the philosophy of the Port Stanley defence – what was considered the 'ground of tactical importance' or 'vital ground' (Staff College terms).

I told him that I already had this information: it was the Sapper Hill and Mount Tumbledown configuration. However, I had a newly captured infantry Major and I said that I would verify this as quickly as possible. I ran back to his headquarters about twenty minutes later with the confirmation.

By coincidence, a Force Intelligence Staff Captain had called at our sheds at this time. He bleated about the fact that my team was a Force asset and I must not be tasked by the brigades, or any lesser formation, unless I went through his office. It gave me great pleasure, at the time, to ignore him. As far as I was concerned, I would deny those close to the front nothing that I knew of or could find out. I felt that we had sufficient common sense among us to be cautious of the dangers of spurious Intelligence.

It was just after I arrived at Fitzroy that I became aware of a dissemination of Intelligence problem that I, if I was careful, could help with.

Infantry officers of various ranks started calling on me: 'We know that even back at the beachhead you were getting good stuff out of these blokes, but why aren't we hearing about it?' was the standard remark. 'Back at Battalion, we've only had a few "Int" signals and the info is mostly as old as the bloody hills!'

It occurred to me what must be happening, and, as with so many apparent hold-ups during the war, no one was to blame. People were being as correct as their written orders required them to be. The problem with the Falklands War was that, because there was rather a lot of dash, inspiration and bravery about, it was racing forward very much faster than these kind of things can do.

I knew all the Intelligence Corps officers in the Force and, without exception, they were very professional operators, particularly the Senior Intelligence Officer. However, they would be deemed irresponsible if they passed forward to the fighting units any Intelligence of the enemy that was not 'hard' – that is to say, Intelligence that had been double-checked to ensure that it was as true as could be known. Only if the same piece of information comes from several non-conferring parties (eg: special forces patrols, air reconnaissance, Interrogators or other sources) can it truly be said to be 'hard'. This careful and correct process, of course, takes a lot of work and time.

It was then that I took the responsibility of deciding to get all I could to the units about to go into action as soon as possible.

Of course I sent everything to the Force Intelligence cell as soon as I got it, but I would also get Unit IOs to come to me or I would go to them, if it was practicable. We would talk through what I had got:

'These minefields I have marked I got from an older Major from Two Sisters. He is a father of teenage sons and is distressed by the young men he has seen killed. I persuaded him to help me stop a few more young men of both sides being killed by showing me the location of as many minefields as he knows in the greater Stanley area. I think that all this is genuine.' Or: 'A slippery little toe-rag of a junior officer reckons that they have got hundreds of Panhards behind the crest of every hill round Stanley. I think he was just trying to impress or say what he thought I wanted to hear; but at least your CO can "worst case" it in his plans.'

In this vein we would quickly and, I think, responsibly go over my team's latest findings.

On the last afternoon of the fighting a full Colonel, the Force's Chief Engineer and an extremely busy man, took the trouble to walk several miles about the forward area until he found me, as by that time I was a constantly foot-mobile Interrogator, so that he could personally express his thanks for mine types and minefields discovered. It had all proved true and we had done, in a small way, what we most wanted to do: save our friends' lives, help the attacks and shorten the war.

At about 1300hrs on 8 June, 1982, I do not remember hearing the air raid warning 'Red' or 'Immediate', but, as our current set of sheep sheds now had 'P de G' on the roof and was theoretically a 'safe' area, and my unit had no radio set of its own, we often heard about these things slightly after the event. However, I did hear the jets over the harbour and some muffled explosions. I realized that an air raid had occurred, but it sounded as if they had bombed Bluff Cove where the Scots Guards were well dug in and should be safe. I was going to enquire what had happened as soon as I could leave the sheds. I had been stuck in the place all day, as was usual. Packets of prisoners were constantly arriving in dribs and drabs and, in any spare moments, I would return to document translating. They just might contain something crucial. I had not even had the chance to see that another landing ship had arrived in the harbour, the RFA *Sir Galahad*.

About fifteen minutes after the raid the Flight Sergeant had to go out on business and the Sergeant asked if he might go with him. They said that they would try to find out the results, if any, of the attack. We could be a bit more mobile at this location as 5 Brigade had a Royal Military Police Unit that took care of the security of the POWs.

Another fifteen-minute period passed and the human noise outside seemed to be increasing. I thought I could hear many voices raised in urgent shouting, the sounds of ever more helicopters arriving and a roaring or rumbling some way off. Were they secondary explosions? I decided that, although I had said that at least one of our three must be with the POWs at all times, I just had to find out what was going on.

I came out of the gloomy sheds into the blinding light of a clear and chilly Falklands day and looked across the narrow walkway bridge to Bluff Cove. It looked quiet, as did the area of the settlement in the immediate vicinity, but there was a terrific lot of noise that I could not seem to orientate myself to for a few moments.

A soldier had the job of running a priceless non-stop tea and slices of margarine-bread table just outside the main shed entrance. I picked up a plastic mug of tea and then looked at his face. He was looking past me in distress.

During the next few seconds, as I turned round, the tea mug flew from my hand and I was running for all I was worth down to the foreshore. I saw one of the most terrible sights that I have seen during five campaigns.

Further down towards the sea end of the harbour, where I had not initially looked, was a huge, violent pillar of red fire, constantly errupting bright orange and yellow flashes of secondary explosion and a giant block of churning black poisonous smoke, so thick it looked solid. Men still moved about in it.

Three bombs had hit the *Sir Galahad* and had exploded at her core, which had been packed with Welsh Guardsmen. The ship still stood on the water, but looked like a sieve. The force of the explosions must have opened up her metal plates as the horrible black smoke poured out of every level of her side; there was also a big hole down near the water line. The thick metal there was punched outwards like tinfoil.

Smoke also trailed from the *Sir Tristram* which floated a hundred metres or so behind the *Sir Galahad*. We later heard that she had been hit by two bombs. She suffered infinitely less damage, but two Hong Kong Chinese members of her crew were killed.

Men were already on the sea in the big orange life rafts and the life boats. Mercifully, that drill seemed to have happened very quickly. There were also men in the water being helped. Unbelievably, helicopters were disappearing again and again into the smoke. They hovered in that, surely, unbreathable atmosphere while trapped men got into, or were put into, harnesses and winched down to the emergency craft.

It must have been impossible to see the ship's superstructure and the many obstacles that could have struck their rotors and sent them spinning to their deaths, but they would not give up. An orange raft, packed with survivors, started to drift back into the flames coming from low down on the *Sir Galahad*'s side so a pilot, as quick-witted as he was brave, descended to the glowing metal and used his down-draught to push the infantrymen to safety. Predictably, the Doctors and Medics from 16 Field Ambulance stayed to the last on the burning ship, amid exploding ammunition, and gave every care they could to the wounded. Many of them were also badly burned, but they worked on regardless.

Everyone who could possibly get away from their war tasks was at the water's edge, helping the bewildered survivors ashore. There were terrible burns and maimings; half a face looked as if it were gone, some men had a missing hand or foot. The fire ball in the area below decks had apparently melted flesh and set hair and clothing on fire within seconds. The battalion of Foot Guards had instantly had 150 men taken from their strength. Forty-eight died and many of the other casualties will require a lifetime of medical care.

After the war I read that the Fuerza Aerea officer who led the five Skyhawks in the bomb attack was very young and it was his first action. His superior had to turn back with a mechanical fault to his aircraft, and the young officer took over. He gave us our worst setback of the war. However, we had already caused even greater casualties with the *Belgrano* sinking and we had certainly killed a lot of his friends in their aircraft. There was, of course, a total acceptance among the British that a military man had to get on with his job. However, there was a strong feeling at the time that someone, or some persons, on our side had behaved wrongly.

The main thing that there seems no doubt about is that troops should not have remained for several hours on board a ship on a clear day when it was common knowledge that the enemy could be a serious air threat. There have been various accounts since the event and, I am sure, the Ministry of Defence has held some thorough investigations.

It has been said that the Guardsmen would not or could not get off because they were still recovering from a particularly bad soaking, they were not in quite the right place to disembark, the *Sir Galahad* unloading ramp stuck, or there were insufficient ferrying craft (LCUs) around. The Senior Army Officer on board might know what happened. However, there were other seniors about, not from the Guards party, who also had authority over events.

The Argentines dug in on Mount Harriet, 10 miles away, had spotted the *Sir Tristram* the day before the fatal raid and had got the information radioed to Argentina. They also subsequently let their air force planners know that a second British vessel had joined the first and so there were now two sitting ducks for them.

It seemed to me that the Guards battalions had the disadvantage of having to get finally and fully adapted 'on the job'. They achieved this admirably. One got the impression that ex-Guards Officers in high places, and there are always many, had used their influence to ensure that their Division was represented. One of the battalions that went to the war came from training and camp duties and the other from ceremonial tasks. About one month after their call-up they were in vicious battles in particularly hostile climate and terrain. Effectively, they only had one fine weather exercise with 5 Infantry Brigade by way of specific preparation.

They are, of course, fully trained infantrymen with an enviable historic record, style and spirit. However, at the time, their war role was as Armoured Personnel Carrier-borne troops, not exclusively foot-moving soldiers like those of the Royal Marines and the Parachute Regiment, when they are not jumping out of small boats and aircraft respectively, and the Brigade of Gurkhas.

If I had been a member of one of the Guards battalions, I might have felt somewhat hastily 'thrown in at the deep end'. Misfortune, in the form of suddenly deteriorating weather and sea, landing craft that broke down and the tragedy at Bluff Cove beset them. Neither were elements of the Task Force too pleased with the Guardsmen, as it was said that they swapped their soaking clothing with dry garments plundered from the ship-stored kitbags of others.

However, men of both battalions, and particularly the Scots Guards, fought two of the hardest days of the campaign. Their enemies were the best regulars the Argentines had and they were well dug in on a steep, jagged feature. Their victory was the final stroke that brought the Argentines to their knees and liberated the Falkland Islanders.

Flushed with success, the Argentine air force made a second attack on our area that day, but they did not have the exceptional luck that they had on the first. Four Skyhawks roared over our main position at Fitzroy. They were greeted by a wall of infantry machine-gun fire and several Rapier missiles. No aircraft were brought down but it was subsequently confirmed from Argentine sources that all were so seriously damaged that their repair time kept them from further participation in the war.

My team and I, as always during air-raids, stayed with our captive foreign charges, ensured that they were as well protected as possible and let them know what was happening. We were, usually, only aware of events by sound and vibration.

The last raid of the Fuerza Airea's Great Day was sad for both sides, and for myself personally. Again four Skyhawks attacked. This time they found a small British landing craft in Choiseul Sound, which is near Goose Green and Darwin, and all but destroyed it with a bomb and cannon fire. I knew all six who were killed on it from the long journey to the war. One of them, a constantly helpful, cheerful and humorous Royal Signals Officer, had become a particular friend. We were going to keep in touch when it was all over and regularly meet up for a beer and a few laughs.

Sea Harriers spotted the attack and turned three of the four Skyhawks into fireballs, killing their pilots. The fourth pilot had lost so much fuel on evasive flying that, if he had not met up with an Argentine tanker aircraft, he would not have made it home. A post-war Argentine account of the actions on 8 June, 1982, describes him, not surprisingly, as 'very shaken'.

All the Argentinians won from the *Sir Galahad* day was a forty-eight-hour delay of their final and humiliating defeat, which was the time it took the British command to reorganize and redeploy their infantry.

In general life for the Interrogation unit at Fitzroy and Bluff Cove continued, for a few more days, in more or less the pattern set upon our arrival. There were more air-raid warnings both false and true, but until 12 June there was not one that alarmed us too much. The numbers of our prisoners gradually increased by more small groups picked up by patrols, then in much bigger numbers once the battles with the Argentines' outermost ring of Port Stanley defensive positions began.

I regularly lost my two NCOs either collectively or individually for a few hours or a day when they were helicoptered over to 3 Commando Brigade, or anywhere else, where a prisoner, still in 'the shock of capture', would respond to a bit of instant and intensive Tactical Questioning (TQ is a shorter and sharper battle version of Interrogation). No one got much sleep but morale was good because we were busy and there were constant signs, albeit they were slow on some days, that we were moving forward to an ultimate victory.

There were still British servicemen who could not understand about Interrogation and what it did. One of the most notable was a 5 Brigade Royal Military Policeman who insolently asked if I would stop talking all night to an Argentine Major in a little room off the sheep sheds, as it would make a cosy little bedroom for him. He was mortified when I told him that if he uttered one more word he would be under Close Arrest and into a sheep pen like a POW.

Until 12 June, 1982, when my unit was scattered across the front to give quick local TQ cover, I remained as the anchor Interrgoator at Fitzroy and Bluff Cove. Also, as an officer, I was the overall POW administrator. However, we were never as misused on lowly POW-related tasks as we had been at San Carlos and Ajax Bay.

The infantry at our location, starting with 2 Battalion of The Parachute Regiment, began moving out en masse on 10 June. That noble Battalion, which so far had had everything the hardest way, disappeared over Bluff Cove ridge and off towards outer Port Stanley in helicopter loads for this, nearly the last, move.

Early on 12 June our sheep sheds suddenly started to fill up with the defeated from Mount Longdon, Two Sisters and Mount Harriet. That morning the three of us worked our way through the relatively few officers that were taken on these outer Stanley features and got useful information on the remaining enemy positions near the capital; then, in the late morning, I lost the two NCOs. Interrogators/TQs were definitely going to be needed forward soon.

I worked on until mid-afternoon, but, although we did not have exact numbers down to the last man, I did not think that there was too much of importance that our field commanders did not know about the remaining enemy-held positions. I confirmed, and recon-firmed, things that we had already discovered.

As the light was just starting to fade from that long day, I got an order from a Force Staff Officer to march with a Royal Marines' field Intelligence cell. My objective was Port Stanley as soon I was able to get into it. My aim when, or if, I made it was to discover as quickly as possible, by getting documents from Argentine HQs, interrogation or whatever, what were the enemy's future intentions for a retaken Port Stanley. Would they bomb it, drop airborne troops into it or what?

My route was from Bluff Cove ridge, via Mount Harriet, Mount Tumbledown, Sapper Hill and Port Stanley racecourse. I knew that I had to be close up with the infantry, as they took the last few positions, and especially for the anticipated street fighting, as my Spanish would be needed. This final phase was particularly disliked by the entire Force. There was a great worry for the lives and property of the fellow Britons whom we had come so far to help.

No matter what might befall, I was elated to be a field soldier again. As quickly as I could, I put on my full webbing, including my small comfortable South Vietnamese army pack with the Argentine exten-sions. I clamp my looted steel helmet on to the top of this bundle with some of my many elasticated bungees that had not initially been mine, and covered the whole package with a piece of stretch camou-flage netting that had once adorned the enemy HQ bunker at Goose Green.

Someone let me use a bit of dark face cream out of their tin and, with my sub-machine gun held at the ready, I set off at the quick march to where the two Commando NCOs awaited me on Bluff Cove Ridge. I also had my portable typewriter attached to the back of my pack.

I had a bit of a look for it in the middle of the night, when I noticed that it was missing, by the inconsistent light from the battlefield illuminations. However, I think that it must have fallen off back near Bluff Cove Ridge as I tripped about in the pitch black or dived into waterlogged fissures at the sounds of nearby ordnance.

My companions were an Army Intelligence Corps SNCO, on a tour of duty with the Royal Marines, and an Intelligence-trained Royal Marine Corporal. They were both lean and fit-looking men, and the Corporal had a radio set. This was likely to prove very useful, as we were unlikely to have a simple ten-mile walk, even assuming that the inner-ring Argentine positions fell. I was at one point called back to a briefing at General Moore's forward headquarters on Bluff Cove Ridge. Fortunately I did not have to do all this on foot, as I managed to get a bit of unofficial helicopter help.

The British assaults on the last Argentine defences before Port Stanley were meant to start on the night of 12 June. However, there was a delay and, as we were foot mobile, we could not discover for certain when they might happen.

The country ahead of us constantly echoed and reverberated with the sound of spasmodic warlike noises: the shellings and mortarings by both sides, the 'thud-thud' of the Argentine heavy machine guns and sudden eruptions of massed small-arms fire. It was impossible to divine precisely what was happening.

We spent a night that was almost constantly lit in some part by parachute magnesium illumination rounds on the edge of a Commando-held position near Mount Harriet. We stayed fully kitted, but wrapped our ponchos and sleeping bags around us for a bit of warmth. The sub-Antarctic autumn had now definitely turned to winter. Snow fell but little settled, as it was whipped away by the violent gale. We managed to snatch the odd period of uneasy sleep.

Just before dawn on the previous day my two companions had heard a sound that they had never heard before, and, I gathered, one that they did not want to hear again. A harsh and vicious roar had risen above the other battle sounds. The noise put a chill into their hearts that was different from anything they had previously felt during the war. From their defensive position just forward of Bluff Cove ridge they had peered anxiously into the flickering, rumbling darkness to their front.

One had pulled the other round and pointed at a great jet of flame that traversed the south-west. HMS *Glamorgan* became the Exocet's last victim that night.

The Officer of the Watch spotted the tail flame and, with one of the best instant reactions of the war, turned the ship's solid stern towards the approaching missile. The giant rocket skidded along the deck and slammed into the helicopter hangar and then on into the galley. Thirteen sailors died and twenty-two were injured. However, things could have been very much worse if the Exocet had gone through the vessel's side and if its warhead had not failed to explode. The *Glamorgan* had been in coastal waters because she was giving gunfire assistance to the troops.

When 13 June dawned we had a quick wash and shave and some breakfast of dry biscuits, jam out of a tube and a bit of warmed up ham and egg mix out of a tin. I made the tea; my NCOs were terribly impressed with the Darjeeling with just a dash of Earl Grey, and I set off, with the Commandos escorting, to see if anyone had need of the Spanish language.

The daylight brought a rapid escalation of artillery noise. The thirty 105mm British guns were firing from within the hills just behind and to the north of us and the big Argentine 155mms fired from Stanley itself. To hear the oscillating whistling or the express train noise, as dictated by the calibre, crossing the sky took me, almost nostalgically, back to the Vietnam and Kashmir wars. We saw the eruption of mud and rock, the drift of grey smoke and then heard the ripping 'crump' of Argentine shells landing about the hill features that our infantry had captured a day ago. I got the occasional scent of my newly commissioned Gunner youth – burnt cordite. Mercifully, the soggy peat soil absorbed much of the tearing shrapnel that the large enemy shells blew out when they burst.

However, the steady build-up of artillery killed and wounded, ours and theirs, carried on. Our bigger helicopters brought up heavy bundles of every necessity for the teeth arms' preparations and the little Gazelles dashed about transporting the casualties.

At one helicopter point there was a young Marine with a piece of sharp, jagged metal in his groin. He seemed to be more comfortable sitting on a rock, rather than lying down, as he waited for evacuation. His friends supported him from either side and gripped him whenever he shook with regular spasms of pain.

It was a very cold day, but crisp and bright, and the clear air of sub-Antarctica seems to create the best visibility I have ever encountered. With the naked eye I am sure that I could see every fissure and hue of even the most distant mountain sides and could have counted the blades of grass on their tussock clumps, had I had time for such things. It must have been an ideal day for artillery observers.

I made a mistake and learned a lesson that I should have known already, after a month's fairly close association with the Argentine character. On one occasion I did not see the need to 'have a dog and bark myself' so to speak, so I told an Argentine Lieutenant to get a motley group of POWs from various units to line up so that, if we got the Sea King helicopter that we were hoping for, they could be got on board quickly.

He used the occasion to give an endless-seeming patriotic propaganda speech in ringing tones. He told the Argentine soldiers what magnificent warriors they were and how right and glorious was their cause. He finally told them to line up where I had said.

Short of shooting him, it would have been difficult to turn his noise off. For the rest of the war I gave almost all instructions to massed prisoners myself. The Argentine officers were just too fond of their own voices, particularly when their egos had taken a bruising.

However, on that occasion, and until the enemy soldiers disappeared on the repatriation ships, I got a very strong impression that by the end the NCOs realized that they had been lied to and they were the ones who had had to take almost all the punishment for national vanity and a pointless adventure. They would never say that out loud, of course; no one in Argentina ever would.

We had a long, physical but worthwhile and therefore quite satisfying day. Mostly, I helped get POWs moved to Fitzroy and did a bit of administrative Spanish speaking that various units needed and some quick TQ here and there; confirmation of the defeated enemy's units and a few details of the Argentine side of events that were useful to the victors. We partly jogged and partly yomped/tabbed up and down, north and south, between locations. One place would tell another, by radio, that we were around if needed. My Intelligence Corps Sergeant had some general questions of the enemy that he deemed important and, when I got the answers to these, I actually had a unit radio set to send them, encoded, back to Force headquarters. We dined on plain biscuits and little packets of dried fruit as we moved or worked.

That day, 13 June, 1982, one of comparative lull between two periods of the most intensive fighting of the war on land, has left me some images as clear and as sharp as nature made the weather for those few moments of history: how dirty, ragged and tired, but positive, 'unmoved and uncomplaining' were my countrymen among the rock, wet earth, heather and tussock, and how young most of them were.

When I had a moment or two between jobs, I would try, figuratively, to stand back and photograph the scenes on to my memory. Garbed in the British bulky camouflage, green webbing and muddied and scuffed black leather boots and gloves and bearing the array of British weapons of those days, and against the backdrop of the sounds and scenes of battle, men efficiently got on with whatever they needed to be doing in a matter-of-fact way. There was humour often, and humanity always.

There we all were, green, maroon and khaki berets, and my blue-grey one. We encountered a party of Gurkhas. The short and strong men were carrying loads, probably mortar parts, across that rough terrain that were as big as themselves.

One could believe that if our Commander had told his fighting troops that the theatre had now shifted and they were to go, as they were, and attack a heavily fortified position at the South Pole, although curious, they would have gone straight away and 'without a quickened breath'.

I wonder how many of the men that I met on that day were not alive twenty-four hours later. All must have been visited, on several recent occasions, by the thought that they might not see too much more of this troubled world.

We heard of activity planned for that night, but, with our peripheral status, we only heard things conversationally from middle or lower levels of the rank structure. One never felt totally positive about things until they happened. The South Atlantic war was, after all, the 'rumour' war!

I knew my eventual mission. Until the situation was such that I could achieve it, I had to stay watchful, stay in communication with events, be helpful if asked and, for now, keep out of the way of those who had difficult tasks ahead. I, therefore, with the permission of the holding force, moved back towards our little natural depression in the ground by Mount Harriet as night started to fall.

Foot movement in the Falklands is, of course, notoriously slow. One constantly has to bend the knee and lift the feet high to climb over awkward tussock clumps. It seemed to take forever to get to our night spot. We were also fairly tired. At last light I had a final clear look at the row of enemy-held peaks about a mile away in the Stanley direction and, with my map, tried in the fading light to reconfirm to myself which one was which. The early British pioneers had given them odd names, I thought.

The confused warlike noises did not stop with darkness; helicopters still rattled about, the shells or mortar rounds still thudded within the hills and valleys and streams of tracer drifted between the peaks. The little 'rat-tat' floated to us a while later.

By late evening we were not far from our night harbour and were looking forward to a brew and a hot meal, if we could achieve such things without causing dangerous light. I had decided that, after our day, what we needed was a good mug from my stronger tea-bags. I had a full-flavoured English mix, but I might put a bit of China with it for subtlety. The problem had been quite agreeably distracting me from my body for the last few miles.

Then the darkness to our front suddenly erupted into a breathtaking firework display of machine-gun tracer. The cacophony of sound reached us a few seconds later. The tiny flicking light specks poured about the dark mass to our front. It looked as if thousands of weapons must be in action. Balls of fire under parachutes were drifting down to the furious activity and there were eruptions of oily explosion on the ground. Bigger flashes of light occasionally streaked across the darkness as if recoilless weapons or light armoured rounds were being fired.

The Royal Artillery batteries on Mount Kent changed to intensive-rate fire. I knew well the furious activity there: the bellow of fire orders, the scream of confirmatory repetition before the echo was gone, shells being driven into breeches, the breeches slammed shut, the explosive roar and rush and the metallic ring of the recoil.

Then, offshore, the guns of the *Yarmouth*, the *Active* and the *Ambuscade* opened up in support of the land troops. We started running towards the sound of the machine guns. The Battle of Tumbledown had begun.

C. Port Stanley and the Reckoning

The back of the Stegosaurus is the shape of Mount Tumbledown, or so I think. It is a rocky ridge a mile and a half long, but very narrow and steep-sided along its flanks. Its length starts from the valley floor to the west and curves gradually up to a hump, 750 feet high, around its centre. It then curves down again as it goes towards Port Stanley and the creature's head submerges in the ground just to the north-west of Sapper Hill.

Thus, the monster lies in a straight east/west line. The Second Battalion of The Scots Guards made their main attack from the tip of the tail, in the west, and up on to, and along, the back. The Argentine regular Fifth Marine Regiment and some Army troops were in well-fortified positions between the beast's spines, or the rock outcrops that went in a line along the ridge. It is the type of ground that overwhelmingly favours the defenders.

To have attacked up the short steep sides would probably have been suicidal, for, while troops made this slow struggle, an enemy on the ends of the ridge would have them in enfilade and could decimate them. The long slow axis, therefore, was the only practicable one. The story of the Battle of Tumbledown is of a physically shattering, eight-hour, sometimes daunting, hand-to-hand fighting slog from one mini-fortress to the next.

That attackers should outnumber protected defenders by a minimum of three to one is the most basic teaching of every tactics school. The Guards had to attack a mainly professional force that equalled them in numbers.

'Fighting through' an enemy-held area is one of the most wearing activities devised by man, even on the easiest type of terrain. It would have been difficult for the British infantry in the Falklands campaign to have had things worse. They inevitably fought up open, steep, boggy, tussock-covered and rock-scattered slopes in wet, windy and freezing weather. The night of 13-14 June, 1982, must have seemed without end to the Guardsmen.

Each platoon, or section, had a soldier who was deemed the most skilled with the 66mm, one-shot-only, hand-held anti-tank weapon. He would take up the best fire position available and his companions would pass the several spare weapons that each of them carried forward to him. He repeatedly blasted the Argentine 'anchor' heavy machine-gun post in the particular rock 'fort' that currently faced them. When it appeared to have been silenced, the big Guardsmen took the position as their ancestors of the past three hundred years would have done — by physical assault and the bayonet.

The British Army is one of the few that in this century still give this ancient weapon a place. It seems to be no bad thing, as our enemies are usually induced to develop an abhorrence for it and its user. It was probably because of these old-fashioned-style final assaults, junior officers leading soldiers in a bayonet charge, that many media reporters were put in mind of earlier British wars, and in that countryside, the Crimea in particular.

At about 0230 in the morning, about six hours after it started, the

Guards' attack seemed to be slowing. Fortunately, in times of crisis, someone is sent. On this occasion it was Major John Kiszely, the officer who had played beautiful airs of his homeland during his last moments of peace. He led all those around him in a bayonet charge up the long fire-raked hillside and through the layers of well-prepared Argentine positions. When he finally reached the top the day was won for the Scots Guards. Every man who accompanied him had fallen dead or wounded, or struggled, wounded, to stay with their officer.

These were Praetorians, the selected personal protectors of a Sovereign. They might not have physical fitness as a training priority, like Marines and Paras, but their responsibility to history and their position was awesome. No matter how many of them fell, they knew that there could be no outcome but victory.

By coincidence I met John Kiszely just after the battle. He uttered not a word of how hard had been the ordeal, of his heroism, that was already becoming the talk of the day, or of the bullet that had hit him. His only care was for those who had been lost.

During that night of non-stop battle my group waited at the ready in case a call came. The 'overs' and 'unders' screamed or sighed by. However, nothing could have distracted us from the events to our front.

A few days earlier I had suggested to my old acquaintance, Brigadier Tony Wilson, that, as most Argentine enigmas were now known, would I not be better employed as an infantry officer? He had turned me down in his usual firm, but light-mannered, way. He assured me that there was nothing personal about his decision, as there was absolutely no reason why I, as an individual, was especially worth preserving. However, the Force was so short of Spanish-speakers that, sadly, they just could not risk arbitrarily throwing one away.

He told me not to feel so bad about being an Interrogator and we should have some champagne together when the war was won and be glad that everyone had done whatever they had to do to gain the victory.

I bought two bottles of champagne from a ship's store in Port Stanley on that great day, but the Brigadier had to be at Fitzroy, where his Command was gathered, and I could not get to him. I therefore felt it fitting to give the bottles to a family of Falkland Islander friends so that they could toast their deliverance in style. I finally met up with the Brigadier again on the steps of St Paul's Cathedral.

Concurrent with the Scots Guards' assault along Mount Tumbledown, the 'men of the match', the Second Battalion of The Parachute Regiment, were fighting an action nearly as fierce some two miles to the north, as they cleared the length of the two parallel features known as Wireless Ridge.

The new Commanding Officer of the victors of Darwin/Goose Green was determined that his men should not have to take another position by little more than their hand-held weapons and their bodies. For 2 Paras' second battle he got his wish. The Battle of Wireless Ridge has become famous as the main 'all arms' battle of the war. Naval gunfire support, artillery, the guns of the Blues and Royals' light tanks and battalion and additional mortars supported his men this time. The Argentine bunkers were as strongly constructed as usual, the ridges were defended by an Argentine parachute regiment and the Paras did not have everything easy, but the well-proven unit rolled the enemy up before them during that night.

From my position I could see no detail of this action. The area, and its light and sound display, were masked and confused by the bulk of Tumbledown.

The Parachute Battalion mortars fired so many rounds that night that the base-plates became unstable on the boggy ground. To ensure that their friends continued to get the life-saving fire support, men of the mortar detachments held the base-plates steady by standing on them. They knew that the jolt of the firing could break their ankles.

Two nights earlier, while I had still been at Fitzroy, the outer ring of Argentine high-feature fortifications had fallen to the British: Mount Longdon, Two Sisters and Mount Harriet.

The battle for Mount Longdon had been the most costly British victory of the war and one of the hardest fought. The attacking Third Battalion of The Parachute Regiment came up against predominantly Argentine regular marines, who nearly equalled them in number, who had half-a-dozen well-sited, fortified and defended heavy-machine-gun positions and plenty of fire support. It too had been a night of ceaseless, often bayonet, battle along the length of a west-to-east ridge through one tough 'fortress' after another.

The ferocity of the battle is shown by the fact that some 3 Para companies had fifty per cent casualties and a Victoria Cross was awarded to Sergeant Ian McKay, the only award of the highest British decoration for the Port Stanley battles. An Argentine heavy machine gun and its defending unit of infantry held up 3 Paras' attack. Sergeant

McKay destroyed it. Once again a lone Para gave inspiration when it was desperately needed, and once againit was at the cost of his life.

The attack on the Two Sisters, so called because of its twin east and west peaks and saddle in between, had begun just after the battle for Mount Longdon had started and was made by 45 Commando, Royal Marines. They assaulted up two sides of the western 'turret' simultaneously, and about twenty-four hours after the end of their 70-mile 'yomp' from San Carlos. They had good Royal Artillery and Royal Navy gunfire support and, despite the heavy weight of machine-gun fire put down onto their approach by the two defending Argentine infantry companies, they prevailed without too many casualties. Once the western peak was taken, the enemy left the eastern peak and fell back to Tumbledown.

Though most of 11 June British attacks on this circle of hills overlapped, the Mount Harriet was the last to start, by a short while. 42 Commando startled the defenders of this steep, isolated and compact rocky mass by attacking them from behind. The Royal Marines moved silently round to the south of the position during the early dark, negotiated a minefield, and, still in silence, swarmed up the eastern side of the feature and in among the Argentine positions.

Individual Argentinians behaved bravely during the rest of that night. However, the Commando CO's clever plan had thrown the defending 4th Regiment into near chaos. Some attempts were made to reorganize the defence during the battle and to counter-attack but, with the dawn of 12 June, the defence collapsed. The Argentines had also been on the receiving end of one of the biggest Royal Artillery pre-assault barrages since the end of the Second World War. The originality, speed, resolution and fire support of the attack also kept British casualties light at the battle for Mount Harriet.

There was grim satisfaction in one victorious Royal Marine Company as the lightly snow-covered battlefield was contemplated in the grey dawn. They were the men of the old Naval Party 8901 who had made the doomed stand at Government House about ten weeks earlier.

As the frozen day of 14 June gave the very first intimation of itself, with a just discernible paling of the black roof above the dying lights and sounds of Tumbledown, I got an order over my radio to go back to Force tactical headquarters on Bluff Cove Ridge.

My humour at the time, as a forty-year-old who felt as rheumaticky and arthritic as a ninety-year-old after nearly three, often open-air, weeks in the Falklands climate, was not cheered by this news. It was not having to retrace my steps that depressed me, it was the prospect of more repatriation clerical work. I could not imagine that, after this night, there was anything worthwhile that further Interrogation could achieve. I had already been given a valuable Mission, and one that I was eager to get on with!

Some senior administrator was no doubt panicking at the thought of all those foreigners. The many English-speaking Argentine officers would gladly work with our clerks, as they had done at Ajax Bay! The POWs could not wait to be back in the warm of northern Argentina and watching the World Cup.

Peeved, I initially hobbled and then, as I shook off some of the cold and damp, strode purposefully off towards the nearest echelon area to see if there was any space on a returning helicopter. Someone would get a piece of my mind!

On Tumbledown a beaming Argentine junior officer, waving a German sniper rifle with the latest telescopic and night sight, strode out to surrender. He bragged companionably to a group of Guards officers that he had brought down eight Guardsmen that night.

Anxiously murmuring things like 'Geneva Convention', a few Battalion officers had to hang on to the Commanding Officer's pistol hand for a moment or two.

'White flags!' was the phrase going from group to group of British servicemen on the approach to General Moore's forward headquarters.

The Guards' victory was probably the final blow that sent the Argentine position, which many dogged Britons had already got into irrevocable slide, on its final chute. As the battle for Tumbledown came to a close, screaming, blade-waving Gurkhas, of 1/7th The Duke of Edinburgh's Own Gurkha Rifles, charged up Mount William and The Welsh Guards, reinforced by companies from 40 Commando, Royal Marines, hurried up Sapper Hill. The Argentine units on these features, which were almost part of Port Stanley, had seen every one of their other positions fall and, after a few fusillades at their attackers, started to stream back into the town and on to the airfield.

For a few hours it was not yet over for the Argentine forces. The fleeing troops had to run a gauntlet of artillery fire, bombs, air-to-ground missiles, air-to-ground strafings, light tank and long-distance heavy machine-gun fire, and the pistols of some of their own officers who had passed the war as squatters in Port Stanley homes.

In ones and twos, and finally in dozens, white flags went up in and around Port Stanley; the political state of the central South Atlantic, and a large portion of Antarctica, had effectively been decided for the foreseeable future.

40 Commando, Royal Marines, received the surrender of the Argentine garrison on West Falkland a few days after the capitulation at Stanley and parties of Royal Navy and Royal Marines rounded up the Argentine civil servants, who were trespassing on the British Antarctic territories, during the ensuing week.

Few of us get the chance to be present at significant moments of history and be near the principal actors when they occur. However, I did have this privilege, just once.

As I ducked my head down to waist level to shove it, and the rest of me, under the camouflage netting and between the green canvas flaps that formed the entrance to the British Land Force forward tactical headquarters, I nearly cracked foreheads with someone who was coming out in a fairly determined manner. I stood back, as the exiter was further advanced in the action than I. The short and strongly built figure in the green denim field cap that faced me was none other than our Commander himself. He had previously given me a few kind and encouraging words as he had passed, on board HMS *Fearless*, at Ajax Bay and at Fitzroy, as he did with every one of us when he could. The snap and style of my Attention and Salute could, I hope, have got me a job as the photographic model in the Drill Pamphlet.

'I've just heard that there may be some good news, Sir,' I said in a chirpy way.

'White flags over Stanley,' he answered quietly.

Before I knew it I had burst out impertinently, 'Gosh, jolly well done, Sir! Thank you very much!'

As I uttered my inane remark I realized that he was leaving his headquarters for a while to take a stroll away from the others. With luck, no more of his, or the Argentines' young men were going to die.

My departing salute was just a blur as I hurled myself into the command post. General Sir Jeremy Moore had just given the famous order to his troops that henceforward they were only to open fire in self-defence.

Before I had a chance to decide who was in need of a lecture about the difference between Interrogators and the lesser mortals who associate with POWs, a Staff Lieutenant-Colonel, who appeared to have been waiting for me, called out, 'Ah, good! There you are!' and sprang from behind his table.

He propelled me to a far corner of the chamber and shot glances over both shoulders.

'Look,' he said confidentially, 'obviously, we British, decent, play with a straight bat, that sort of thing. . . . And we would never do anything like . . . take hostages, for example,' he went on. 'However, the old *dagos* have been very naughty and, just by way of a little insurance against their better future behaviour, London wants you to sort out a few – about five hundred – commanders of major units, special forces officers, political animals, technical specialists. You'll know what's wanted, won't you?'

I nodded.

'Good!' He said with an encouraging smile.

'Well, you had better be running along then. I know that you already have an urgent task and, as soon as we can get mass repatriation going and the Argies passing along the jetty to embark, you grab your five hundred. OK?'

I said, 'Yes, Sir,' saluted and left.

While I was waiting for a helicopter to take me forward again, it occurred to me that I should have asked what the policy was if the types that we wanted to retain, until it was certain that Argentina planned no more immediate hostilities, and the figure five hundred did not match up.

By coincidence, in the event they did match up almost exactly. However, just to be on the safe side, as my arithmetic has never been terribly good, I threw in a few extra Captains and Lieutenants.

The Flight Sergeant, the Sergeant and I briefly examined every Argentine still alive on the Falklands, about 12,500, as they shuffled in frozen, malnourished and depressed blocks along the Public Jetty. Those I pulled out of the columns I put first into a Port Stanley warehouse for a few days and then they were helicoptered to Ajax Bay freezing works. They were finally put on board the British Rail ship *St Edmund*.

They had a boring, miserable and humiliating time. The prison ship is known in Argentina as 'the pig pen' (*el Chiquero*) and the episode is one of the most resented of the war. It was particularly distressing to the wives and families of the twelve full Colonels, twenty-five Lieutenant-Colonels, the host of Majors, the technical specialists (some of them non-commissioned), additional Captains and one or two Lieutenants, that I gathered, when the men of other families returned and theirs did not.

I am directly to blame and I am sad that women and, particularly, children were made unhappy by me. However, those Argentinians, morally supported by their wives and grown-up families, had barged into the homes of others, had thrown their weight about, had destroyed and dirtied their property and had definitely distressed and frightened the women and children of the Falklands.

My team was never given access to the very senior Argentine officers. Captain Rod Bell attended to them and they were kept for the extra month on HMS *Fearless*.

A helicopter dropped me off, in the late afternoon of 14 June, 1982, from more or less where I had taken off that morning. I had told the two Commando NCOs to move forward, when they could, and link up with my two usual SNCOs in the town if possible. Optimism that we might get into Port Stanley without destructive street-fighting was growing.

I passed the Port Stanley War Memorial to the First and Second wars and the Secretariat Building in the long shadows of the last light of day. My pack had chosen this last walk across the recent battlefields as the moment to self-destruct and had become an unbalanced, awkward and tiring weight.

'You look knackered,' said a cheerful 2 Para Captain who stood with some of his troops by the harbour edge and looked as fresh as a daisy. I snapped up a bit and gave a companionable wave and smile. The town still swarmed with Argentines, who, surprisingly enough, were still armed.

I had trudged across the recent battlefields avoiding minefields either by using obvious troop routes, checking from my interrogation notes or making local enquiry. The ground was impressively torn up and littered with all kinds of débris from the fighting. British soldiers made themselves comfortable amid the mess and pottered about their work as though they had done nothing out of the ordinary.

I wondered what Ardilla, my first lover, would have thought of these scenes. She unquestionably went along with the national statement, about which there could be no discussion, that the Falklands, or 'las Malvinas', belonged to Argentina.

'I love only *jyou*,' I think she once said in her Latin-American accent during what was probably our only union, before my year younger than her made me boring, or men senior to her became more interesting. Her rich dark hair was spread about a pillow that was on a couch, or perhaps on a rug in front of an English country fireplace. She was a teenage Gina Lollabrigida look-alike.

Her son or nephew might have been one of the young men who carpeted parts of the hillsides I walked across. Maybe her husband or brother was one of the tired Majors that I had kept awake for additional hours at Ajax Bay or Fitzroy.

She would certainly not have loved me on that day. If she ever thinks of our time together, what form do her thoughts and memories take now?

A routed army had swept down from Port Stanley's nearby hills, along its streets and gardens, had poured out of the other, eastern, end and had straggled in thousands along the few miles of road to the airfield.

Apparently, what slowed the British advance on Sebastopol during the Crimean War was not a Russian fighting withdrawal but the piles of weapons, shakos and other equipment that our soldiers fell over. They had been cast away by the peasant soldiers who had fled from the British victories at Alma, Inkerman and Balaclava. The view from where I joined the Moody Brook/Stanley road on that day must have had a very similar aspect.

Every category of Argentine hand-held weapon lay in piles along the roads, on pavements and in front gardens. There were brand new recoilless launchers and their rockets in half-broken-open boxes. One could have amused oneself firing at seagulls at a few hundred pounds a shot. Fused hand-grenades were in heaps, and in rows along the gutters, like spilled oranges at a street market. There were two dead Argentine conscripts lying in the road, probably shot by their own Staff officers. It must have been a bit of a token gesture, in view of the numbers of 'deserters'.

Some of the houses on the western, battlefield, side of Stanley were damaged by shrapnel and bullets. However, on the whole, the town looked reasonably intact and seemed to have come through its ordeal amazingly well. Its white wood cottages put me very much in mind of a New Zealand, probably South Island, country town.

The Argentines billeted in the town must have lived like hippies at a long pop festival. Litter, damage and evidence of slovenly living were everywhere. Islanders stood before their broken front porches and in their débris-filled gardens and beamed at us.

First ashore, first into battle, first at Fitzroy and first into Port Stanley, the men of 2 Para were, I noticed, already exuding charm to local young ladies; another first was possibly imminent. The Paras were also happily driving about, with no obvious destination, in giant Argentine Dodge staff cars and Mercedes jeeps and trucks.

For the moment two armies had just stopped fighting because their war had petered out and elements of both milled about together while they waited for someone to tell them what to do next. There was neither hostility nor friendship; groups of soldiers just walked silently past each other. However, a few Argentine soldiers said, 'Good morning' to me in English, although it was the afternoon.

Formal surrender was being organized, and, once that was done, the Argentines would be disarmed and held on Stanley airfield until repatriation could begin.

On the steps of the Secretariat Building I met a man who was to become a firm friend. Since those turbulent times he and his wife have stayed at my home in England. He was the Harbour Master and Chief Customs Officer of Port Stanley and the Falkland Islands, Leslie Halliday.

During the occupation he had been as surly and as unhelpful as he could to the invaders. However, on this day he had put on his best Royal Navy-style uniform, with the Trinity House cap badge, and was smiling with pleasure at the scene he could contemplate from the top of the tall flight of steps, and especially he smiled at the defeated and bedraggled Argentines who trailed by. He was obviously mentally blowing raspberries and waving two-fingered signs. We caught each other's glance, so I walked over and he came down the steps.

'Thanks for the liberation,' he said and we shook hands.

I jokingly replied that some Royal Marines, the Paras, the Royal Navy and a few others had had a hand in it but basically he had got the right chap. We both roared and I then explained that I had done little and was only here because I spoke Spanish.

'Aha!' he exclaimed. 'Can you tell the Argies who are still in there to stop making a mess?' He pointed through the doorway of the Secretariat. 'It's my office,' he went on, 'and since they first barged in there, you wouldn't believe the mess they've made.'

I put my pack down on the doorstep and strode into the hallway. From there I could see into several of the offices on two floors. Argentine soldiers were still sprawled on chairs, eating biscuits and shedding food wrappers. The response to my fairly polite request to stop making a mess and to get the place cleaned up was totally unexpected. Presumably it was obvious by my manner that I was an officer. Many of the soldiers reacted with near terror; my instruction was relayed from office to office and a furious bustle of sweeping and tidying began.

I had intended to do as I would have done with British servicemen – accord the courtesy of an initial quiet but firm order and only adopt the fascist roar if the reaction was not sufficiently impressive. I formed the impression then, and later in the repatriation lines, that perhaps some Argentine officers tend not to command but to bully.

I accepted Leslie Halliday's kind offer to stay in his spare bedroom if it fitted in with the Force's intentions for my movement and set off to see if either of my groups of NCOs were among the early arrivals in town.

Leslie also told me where I might send a telegram, as it was my Corps' fortieth anniversary day parade a few days hence. It was my intention to send a greetings message that made me briefly a true 'Liberator' – in a fairly small way.

The Cable & Wireless office was a single-storey white building just on the right of the start of Government House drive and not far away. I looked through the glass panel in the door and gave it a tap. A pleasant-looking young man with a neat beard and several very pretty girls emerged apprehensively from various side rooms and came a short way into the main office.

I was pleased that they seemed to be still open this late in the day, so I tried the door handle but it was locked. With a polite smile, I called through the glass asking if there was any chance that I could send a telegram. A look of incredulity came over their faces and the young man unlocked the door.

'You're British?' he asked in astonishment.

I was affronted that anyone should ever ask such a question of me. Could they not tell immediately from my aspect, my posture, the set of my jaw, let alone the Queen's crown on my beret badge? I nodded a bit coolly.

The young people all gathered excitedly about me and, to my amazement, told me that I was the first British serviceman they had seen since the invasion. They were aware that it looked as if the Argentines had lost but they were unsure of the exact state of play and had spent the day with the office locked in case the Argentines were shooting people in a fit of pique.

I told them that, even as we spoke, the final details of the Argentine surrender were being thrashed out. They smiled delightedly at each other. It briefly crossed my mind that the pretty girls might hurl themselves upon me in a grateful delirium of hugs and kisses. I genially braced myself. However, the islanders are not impulsively demonstrative folk.

Everyone competed to tell me their most significant occupation stories. Mostly they were examples of the Argentine officers' rudeness and vanity. After my weeks of frugality, mud and military, these young people were a happy interlude.

Finally, they said that they would send my telegram as soon as everything was fully returned to normal and I departed, waving back at their joyful faces in the windows.

During the course of my lowly post-war tour on the Falklands, I had occasion to telephone the Cable & Wireless office on a business matter. It was obviously the bearded young man who answered and I mentioned the occasion of our first meeting.

'You've got a big moustache,' he gasped excitedly.

I do, of course, have a small and, I have always thought, rather stylish 'Imperial'. After confirming this, I expected him to enthuse over what must have been an historic moment for them all. But, 'You were after a bottle of wine,' was all he said.

I then remembered that my very first line, before I knew that I was a 'liberator', had been to ask if there was a shop where I might buy some bottles of wine. I had wanted them for the Halliday household. Local history and folklore would remember me forever as a sot!

However, my search for wine did bring about my next 'liberation.' I headed, as the young office staff had directed, for the West Store. When I rattled the heavy double doors, it was obvious that they too were bolted, which I decided, after looking at my watch, was hardly surprising. It was well after normal shop hours.

Just as I was setting off to get on with my primary duties, there was a sound behind me of the door being unbolted. An elegant lady in a tweed suit came out onto the steps. She had the look of a manageress of a store of some status. There were other figures, male and female, in the gloom of the interior behind her.

'Oh, please don't go,' she called out, almost plaintively.

'I'm terribly sorry I disturbed you,' I said. 'I realize that it is late.'

'He says he's sorry to disturb us,' the lady screamed and started to dab her eyes.

I was getting very worried that, in some way that was not altogether clear to me, I had caused upset and got ready to back away.

'Come in, come in,' she said and, gathering up a handful of the upper sleeve of my parka, pulled me into the supermarket.

Once again I was the first living embodiment of deliverance! The West Store was a very solid stone building and so, during the last few days of heavy bombardment and fighting around the town, it had been used as a refuge for a number of local families.

Again I heard fascinating, and often infuriating, tales of the occupation. I was introduced to everyone and the lady manageress issued all the adults with drinks from the shelves that we might toast victory. It was another brief, but memorable, moment for me.

A few days later, when Port Stanley was packed with troops, I again called at the West Store to replenish my kind hosts' wine. The queues seemed endless, as, of course, British soldiers were eagerly buying the luxuries of which they had long been deprived.

When I got to my turn at the check-out I greeted the girl assistant like a long-lost brother. However, she only had time to give me a quick smile, as the tightly-packed queue was pressing forward and she could hardly stuff the bundles of notes into the till fast enough – but then restoring 'business as usual' for our fellow Britons was what we had come to do.

I made one other quick call before I got on with my work. I may have been the first 'liberator' in there too. I went into Port Stanley Cathedral. I passed the giant whale rib arch and went through the traditional Anglican doors and into the traditional Anglican interior. The great building was lit, but empty and silent.

I am not a very religious person but this sudden, unexpected and short war had been an event of concentrated dramatic scenes and emotions; so I pondered briefly and said a prayer. I had, of course, taken my beret off as I entered but I could not leave my sub-machine gun and ammunition outside. However, our Christian Crusader ancestors took their weapons into Church to be blessed for the service of God.

For most of that night and throughout the next day I scoured Government House, the Argentine airlines/air force office and every building that I heard from local residents had been used by the enemy command for information on any post-defeat plans that Argentina might have. The enemy senior officers used not to sleep in the same building on consecutive nights, presumably so that a member of our special forces, in black clothing and with a stiletto between his teeth, might not find them.

Despite the fact that the Argentines had destroyed masses of paperwork and technical equipment, I found many interesting documents. However, none of them were concerned with any contingency plans. I therefore suggested to Force headquarters that this was probably only known by the Buenos Aires Junta themselves, if, indeed, any decision on the matter had been reached. I found an Argentine assessment of our SAS. It was an entertaining mix of truth and fancy, so I made a translation and gave it to the senior SAS officer.

Apart from the mess made by the Argentines and the war, the litter of Argentine small arms and field equipment and the mass of armed soldiers of both sides, the most impressive aspect of newly recaptured Port Stanley was the abandoned larger military equipment.

As I hurtled about the town tracking down the buildings that had been used by commanders or communicators, I came across a colossal flat trailer that had been tipped off near a corner of the road to the airfield. Five Exocets, worth then £5/6 million each, had spilled from it. One of the giant ribbed boxes had burst open and a finned Titan tail stuck out. It was from there that the missile that hit HMS *Glamorgan* was fired. Presumably the full complement of the giant trailer that now lay on its side in the ditch was six.

There was a back street full of a squadron's worth of French Panhard armoured cars and the plateau directly above the town, and referred to as 'the common', was littered with some of the finest guns that Europe produces: Italian 105 and French 155 field guns and Swiss Oerliken, German Rheinmetal and Italian 20mm anti-aircraft guns. All the guns were surrounded by considerable quantities of ammunition.

I met the Royal Artillery Commander, a full Colonel, up there. He had some of his Gunners and vehicles with him and was obviously planning the tidy-up and sort-out. I said that, as one of the callings of my Corps was anti-aircraft gunnery, I was sure that we would like to have the Oerlikens. I visualized them as impressive 'ornaments' at the entrances, or main crossroads, of RAF Regiment camps. The Colonel said that I might take charge of the Oerlikens until some higher decision was made about them, but I had to get them cleared away as soon as I could. There were six of the twin long-barrel guns; they weighed several tons each.

I did not, of course, have any time to spend on the guns, as I was required on any remaining Intelligence duties and the impending vast POW repatriation task; neither could I have moved a single gun on my own, as a detachment of men with a towing vehicle would be required for each one. However, I had a plan.

I regularly dealt, on POW supply matters, with an aged, experienced and wily Royal Marine logistician. He could achieve unbelievable things. He would frequently take tea with my reunited unit and myself in the Argentine airlines/air force office which, from 15 June, was our base. As soon as I saw him we quickly and amicably organized passage to Britain for one or two guns. He and some of his men helped me drag the guns up an alley where they might not be spotted and commandeered by anyone else. I pressed upon him some cases of Argentine whisky for his unit's next social function. I had inadvertently discovered them during my Intelligence sift.

Over the next few days, while my tiny team worked almost sleeplessly to check and put on a ship, or in a warehouse, each of the 12,500 or so POWs, I kept an eye out for any members of my Corps' Rapier Squadron. They had had a frustrating war, for although they had a more modern and sophisticated version of the missile system than the Royal Artillery, they had been deployed away from most of the action. However, they had provided defence and boosted morale at the areas they guarded.

After I had been in town for about four days I at last spotted two of the Squadron junior officers on the seafront. I was able to tell them about the guns, where they were and that their sea passage was booked. I introduced them to my Royal Marine friend and they hurried off to fetch a work party and vehicles.

Amazingly, all the Argentine Oerlikons and all the ancilliary and spare parts eventually went back to Britain as RAF Regiment property.

They did not become 'ornaments', as I had envisaged, but were put into perfect working order and went into British service as the equipment of two newly raised reservist units. The inspiration behind this was a well-known, ingenious and energetic Squadron Leader who was, fortunately, in a Staff position where he could make direct suggestions to the highest ranks.

A couple of years after the war I attended the opening of a newly refurbished RAF Regiment Museum and there was a splendid poster of one of the Oerlikons in Port Stanley with the Rapier Squadron Commander and another officer on either side of it. The caption recounted that the Squadron had captured it. This is true enough, as an RAF Regiment Officer was the first of the British forces to get to it and our Corps and its sub-divisions are effectively one.

The commander of our only unit of the war did deservedly well. He was given an award and promotion following the war. When he left the Service he became, by coincidence, a senior official in the local government of my county. He advertised a job on his staff and I telephoned and wrote an application for it. I did not get a reply. Sadly, the old unfair days of ex-wartime comrades being like Mafia or Freemason societies cannot continue in these competitive times.

The Port Stanley Inadvertent Military Reunion along the seafront on 15 June, 1982, was an event as memorable and as impressive, in its way, as some of the warlike happenings.

Until the British forces got fully reorganized after the fighting and, to prevent overcrowding, units were allocated to buildings outside of the capital, though most of the front-line troops managed to get into the town to have a look at the place and the people that they had fought for, and many of their friends had died for.

Because regiments and corps had to be spread about the vessels of the armada for the journey down, and the circumstances upon arrival had dictated a fairly scattered distribution of units, many servicemen had not had the opportunity to meet up with people from outside their current military circle. On the Stanley waterfront men discovered that friends they had been parted from since cadet and recruit days had, theoretically, been at their side during the terrible things that had just passed. Reputedly, the British rarely indulge in pointless and time-wasting displays of emotion. However, on that day many troopers roared with joy and gripped the shoulders of fellows that they had not seen, in some cases, since their boyhoods.

To my amazement I too saw again people who I had previously met in various old Commonwealth armies and who now, hitherto unknown to me, had become Marines, Paras or SAS men. I also discovered that two cousins, whom I had lost touch with since childhood, were in the war: one was a helicopter Navigator and the other, Captain Derek Dalrymple, was a Commando Artillery Forward Observer.

Artillery Fireplans have an identifying nickname and Derek called his last, heaviest and most devastating 'Fire Plan Iron Lady' after the Prime Minister who had remained so steadfast behind the Falkland Islanders and the Task Force.

When he got home he sent her the original Royal Artillery proforma of it and received a personally written note in reply. There was not a question of doubt of how genuinely moved was this strong-spirited woman, who had constantly had to counter the sabotage effects of the weaker British politicians.

The end of the fighting effectively brought an end to the Interrogation unit's role. My tiny force, that had neither a title, a place on any Force list, any kind of official existence, nor would be mentioned by any history of the conflict, was fragmented within a week of the surrender.

Our last week together was an almost sleepless one. The Force's priority was to remove the Argentines from the islands. This was not particularly done on principle or through any feeling of dislike; it was simply that there was insufficient food and accommodation for the British troops, and certainly not enough to support nearly two thousand interlopers as well.

We three, and some interested Royal Marines who had been detached to help us, stood almost consistently on the Port Stanley Public Jetty for six or seven days. There were no other Spanish speakers to do this job. During the night we took it in turns to try and get a couple of hours' sleep on a nearby floor out of the drizzle.

The *Canberra* and the *Norland* and later the Argentine *Bahia Paraiso*, in that order, anchored off the jetty and loaded up with the packets of POWs that small harbour craft ferried out to them. Seemingly endlessly, the broad queues of Argentine soldiers inched by. They were filthy and dispirited. Many looked very ill with malnutrition, hypothermia and influenza. Twenty-four hours a day, from 15 June to about 20 June, the Marines and Paras, who guarded the POWs down at the airfield, marched them the two miles to us in roughly regiment-sized packets.

A Flight Sergeant of my Corps, who was also detached to the Army and was on guard duties at the airfield, told me that he found several conscripts in sad dead bundles in the cockpits of wrecked aircraft and under sheets of corrugated iron where they had tried to escape the eternal wind, cold and damp.

As each Argentine unit arrived, I would tell them to dump all packs and kitbags in a prescribed area, as they would not be taking them on board ship, and I would then get them into the order: soldiers to the front, NCOs and warrant officers next and officers at the rear. Thus, the largest packet that could be quickly dealt with could be got out of the way first, a little more time would be spent on the middle packet and most time on the last packet. It was from this final group, of course, that I selected my nation's 'guests', or whatever they were.

My two NCOs and I stood in a line, with RM and RMP body-searchers around us. We would call a man forward and our escort would disarm him, if he had not already stacked arms somewhere else, take any additional things like officers' pistols, bayonets, sheath knives or anything that, by any stretch of the imagination, could be used to attack a guard or merchant seaman on board a crowded ship.

When this was done, we Spanish-speakers would establish that the POW was who he appeared to be and what his unit was, to ensure that we were still dealing with whom we thought we were. Most cases were quick, simple and obvious. If there appeared to be any ambiguity, we continued the interview until satisfied or put the subject into our guarded warehouse for a second look and possible retention.

I made a mistake before I had developed a quick enough instinct for the task. Almost the first two Argentines of my very first queue were two middle-aged men in uniforms unsoiled by field duty and who had large white plastic crosses attached to the left breast of their combat jackets. They carried a four-foot-high ornate statue of the Madonna, in protective packing, between them.

They said that they were priests. I did not think them very impressive; one had an unpleasant 'yob' face and hairstyle and the other was obese and obsequious. I ordered a thorough search of the statue, in case it was stuffed with anything that we might want to see, and asked for ID cards. They said that, as technical civilians, they were not issued with such things. For some reason I smelt a rat, or two in this case, and should have followed my instinct. However, the queues were backing up and it did not seem worth spending extra time on them. We had won, after all. There was nothing in the statue. I therefore waved them on to the ferrying craft.

The nearly overwhelming tasks of the next few days took the pair from my mind. However, as soon as I had a chance, I described them to Leslie Halliday. 'Yob face' was a vile and cowardly abuser of the helpless of the Astiz type and the bladder of lard had actually been ordained as a priest but was a total traitor to his profession. He was a nasty bullying Argentine propagandist. They were a couple who truly deserved the worst that *el Chiquero* had to offer.

Part of the way through our first repatriation day I suddenly noticed that our Royal Military Policemen were carrying Argentine, United-States-made sub-machine guns instead of their British Sterlings. They were not officially trained on the weapon, nor had they been checked for safety or 'zeroed' to their aim. It was a bit of a pose, to which all young men are prone. However, about the same time that I noticed this silliness, so did someone senior in their organization. The men disappeared briefly and reappeared shortly afterwards with the correct weapons.

I am sure that most British Officers visited us to stare at the amazing sight of such a concentration of defeated military humanity and to have a chat. It was good to see them as I knew almost all of them, at least slightly, either from previous service or from earlier in the current campaign.

Many of them would sneak a pistol from the ever-growing mound of Argentine officers' side arms. The pile got to a size that would easily have filled the floor space of an average living room and about half-way up to the ceiling. Their activity was useful, in that it stopped the collection getting to the stage where it blocked the jetty.

My father was a Royal Navy Gunnery Officer and weapons expert during the Second World War and I remember him saying when I first set off on Imperial service that I should never retain a captured weapon, as it always gets fired in domestic circumstances sooner or later. The hundreds of newspaper stories of children accidentally killing each other in the decades following my father's war have been a tragic testament to his wisdom.

The Force headquarters got wind of this trend and, sadly, officers who had recently been very heroic had the indignity of a kit search and being on the receiving end of a bit of shouted criticism and advice from a superior.

Journalists appeared, both British and Argentine. The British journalists who had been covering the war wanted 'how the Argentines felt about things now' stories. In the interests of good military PR with the Fourth Estate, I acted as interpreter. The Argentines who were interviewed glanced at their listening companions and said that they still thought that it had all been a good idea. I am certain that they did not state their true feelings.

The Argentine journalists were in military uniforms, which they said I should disregard, and waved 'International Press' ID cards at me. I gave all of them the benefit of a month of first-hand experience, researching an in-depth article on *el Chiquero* for their publications. When, after the war, I read the lies that they had been writing about Argentine victories, the irrefutability of their cause and the destruction of the malevolent British and their aircraft carriers, I did not feel quite so bad about things.

For the first eighteen hours there were just too few of us about once the piercing cold and damp night fell. The British military 'tourists' understandably returned to whatever warmth and comfort they had managed to create in their post-conflict harbours. They had been subjected to more than enough exposure to that hard climate.

The tail end of our POW queue staged a minor riot on the night of 15 June and my tiny unit could do nothing about it. One of the stories was that it was the conscripts turning on the Stanley-based 'political' officers who, along with the Junta, had tricked the citizens-in-uniform into the Falklands folly. However, a side-effect of whatever it was for was the looting and burning of a nearby Falklands general store. A Northern Ireland-style twenty-four-hour street patrol resulted.

Argentine units that had taken no part in the fighting now appeared. They had either been deployed to the east of Port Stanley about the airfield and lighthouse peninsula, which was reasonably considered a possible direction of British attack, or on West Falkland. They arrived still full of swagger and self-justification. It seemed to lessen a bit in the jetty queues or the warehouses. But the Argentine 25th Regiment, from east of Stanley, were ordered by one of their officers into a ceremonial 'goose step' for the last few paces up to us to show that they were unbowed.

Sadly, there were a few displays of unlikeable British behaviour. An

Intelligence Corps Staff Sergeant appeared, who, although he was serving with a Commando formation, did not wear their beret. Most attached personnel have a go at the daunting Commando course to be at one with their temporary unit. He seemed to anticipate possible enquiry from the RM members around the jetty by stating, before any question was asked, that his obvious Corps professionalism did not require him to prove himself further. There was no reason to doubt the truth of his statement.

However, although he spoke not a word of Spanish, he took to inserting himself occasionally among the prisoners and making loud mocking laughter in the faces of senior Argentine officers. Presumably he felt that they needed further humiliation and perhaps knew how much the Latin ego would hate that sort of thing. Unfortunately, I witnessed only the final example of his behaviour before he got bored and returned himself to more standard Intelligence duties. My SNCOs told me of other occasions. I told an Intelligence Corps junior officer to keep him away from the POWs, but he too seemed to consider the Argentine senior officers to be well deserving of this and any other insult.

The Royal Military Policemen, who arrived right at the end of the week with the company-sized official POW handling unit, when there were only 500 POWs left, would start their search of POWs by throwing their caps or berets into the nearest muddy puddle. This unit had taken no part in the war. The combat uniforms of its personnel were so crisp and new-looking, compared to the clothing of those who had fought the war, they gave the impression that they wore pyjamas.

For their totally ill-prepared and uncomprehending behaviour towards the wartime British and Argentines about the jetty and warehouses my extended team and I immediately, and perhaps unreasonably, loathed every one of the Johnny-come-lately but officially established POW handling company and their every aspect.

I first became aware of the Major in charge when he bounced up and said, 'Right! Whoever thinks he's in charge here, he's not. I am!'

I congratulated him on his command, told him that my six or so people had done ninety-nine per cent of the work, most POWs were long gone, and, as he obviously wanted a clear field, I would fall my men out. They were ready to drop and, since late May, I had been promising to lay on a small drinks party for them once our duties seemed over. He became both ill-at-ease and friendly and said that he would like my unit to carry on as we were, but with the benefit of the supervision of his professional and properly constructed unit.

The final 500 POWs seemed to take nearly as long to process as the 12,000 who had preceded them.

I suppose that my team had had the advantage of being able, because of the inspiration of constant wartime emergency, to learn the POW business quickly and about the Argentines, and I should have been more understanding of an unfortunate situation. However, I have always been sorry that the members of my unit, who rose so brilliantly to their 'thrown-in-at-the-deep-end/make-and-mend' war, had a pedestrian note at the end.

The new POW unit commander said, shortly after he arrived, that, in view of the speed with which I waved conscripts past, I could be letting colonels dressed in conscript clothing get away. I said that I knew that I was not. The poor Major had not seen the thousands that we had. He could not know that a part-Indian youth, with a vacuous look, was definitely not a colonel.

'This chap,' he said on one occasion, indicating my current conscript, 'could be an officer who has changed clothing and ID with one of his men?'

He seized the conscript's ID disc in such a way that his hand completely hid its details.

'Right! What's your regimental number?' he said in English.

The very dark Argentine teenager looked from one to the other of us in bewilderment.

'*Qué es su numero de matriculaçion?*' I repeated.

The young soldier rattled off a number. It was the number on the disc. A recent impostor would not, of course, have had the time to learn another's regimental number so well.

The Major was trying to be correct according to the training. All he lacked was experience of this particular theatre. I managed to stay silent for the couple of days that we were together.

The Argentine military police unit that passed before us early in the repatriation saga, during the small hours of 16 June, greatly interested us. Argentine military police are not, or were not then, like our military police. Ours are responsible for military internal order, whereas the Argentine version were a type of 'Gestapo' – internal order and political correctness.

It was not the men that interested us, although they were immaculately smart, it was their dogs. They were the biggest and best-kept Alsatians I have ever seen. They were like a cross between a bear and a lion. The six were perfectly behaved with their handlers. However, by unspoken agreement between my men and myself, we did not attempt a body, or fur, search.

I asked one handler if his dog ate 'gringos', as I tentatively reached out to pat the magnificent animal. The policeman was terribly regimental and took me seriously.

'*Non, non, mí Capitan; ninguna problema!*' he said, shocked, and snapped to attention.

A *Cabo* (Corporal), late one night, was clutching a smart square case which obviously made him a marked man. I, and at least two of the RMP, swooped on him. His case contained a beautiful trumpet. Our orders were that the Argentines took nothing off the islands except the clothes they stood up in. The man was a bandsman and very obviously treasured his instrument.

'What if he plays us a tune, Sir?' a sympathetic Royal Military Policeman asked.

I told the soldier of the circumstances under which he and his trumpet might not be parted. He took it from its case and effortlessly trilled a lovely traditional and sentimental Latin American or Spanish air. None of us, British or Argentine, on that filthy, wet and freezing dockside had had the company of any beauty for such a long time. A thousand men fell silent. The Royal Military Policeman gave him a smiling and friendly shove on his way.

The interminable week went on and on; day and night became the same to us. If we wanted to eat, we could usually only take a quick snack of biscuits from our pockets. Once in a while there was some sort of administrative hiccup and we were without POWs for a short while. We would instantly organize into two shifts for a few minutes of tinned ration warm-up in an empty office nearby.

I was delighted when I found a discarded packing case of enemy chocolate. I ate a bar while I worked and, when I went back later for a second, I took the trouble to translate the writing on the box. It was, of course, laxative chocolate.

Certain types of Argentine food packs contained miniature bottles of whisky. I found that one of these taken occasionally kept me more cheerful but, more importantly, seemed to keep me awake.

For the entire week I was ceaselessly under the hate-filled gaze of those of the 'special category' POWs who could get to the window or doorway of the warehouse where they, unknowingly, awaited transportation to Ajax Bay. There must be many vendettas sworn on me.

Many of the famous personalities of the war came to visit the impressive drama that I stage-managed. Major John Kiszely and Major Chris Keeble, who took over at Goose Green and led his Battalion on to victory, passed by. General Moore and a couple of colonels came to inspect and to discuss matters among themselves. Our Land Force Commander gave me an encouraging grin from over a departing shoulder.

Brigadier Julian Thompson, the Commander of 3 Commando Brigade, who could have been a stand-in for the 'Superman' movies, nearly crushed one of my shoulders when he placed a friendly hand on it, and, with a joke and a happy laugh, seemed to confirm more than anything that the grim times were over, or nearly over.

Companies of Royal Marines and the Parachute Regiment marched by, now in corps and regimental berets, on their way to the airfield. They were battlefield worn and torn; they carried giant packs and well-serviced and well-used weapons and radiated unaffected nobility. Some companies carried their standards. I would call my POW workers to attention and a few young infantrymen looked sheepish. They could not seem to realize that they had done anything worthy of admiration.

The Pipes and Drums of the Scots Guards marched and counter-marched through the town one day. Most Falkland Islanders' ancestors come from Scotland and men, women and children marched after the band in delight.

On the day that the POWs were nearly done Captain Rod Bell managed to get away to see us for a short while, from his very important interpreter and liaison duties with General Moore and General Menendez. The significance of the behind-the-scenes work that he did in the war is almost impossible to exaggerate.

His achievements must also be unique in British military history. With, of course, our Force's blessing, he established a clandestine radio link that the Argentine command on the Falklands could, and did, intercept. Speaking nothing but the truth, but by presenting the war situation in such a way that he knew, from his intimate knowledge of the Latin American world, would be respected, he persuaded the Argentines not to continue resistance beyond what was sensible. Rod

Bell is personally and directly responsible for the saving of an inestimable number of young lives.

At Ajax Bay he would speak to senior POWs exactly as an Argentine junior officer would.

'*Si, mí Coronel!*' he would say with a snappy salute. They loved it.

I was delighted to see him because he was great company and I had a matter of post-war business I was anxious to discuss with him. I explained that my main secondary duty at my Corps' Depot was Curator of the Museum and that I had already in my mind's eye worked out a striking display of the Argentine historical and modern military items that I had had the good fortune to gather for posterity. However, what I really needed to perfect the montage was a large Argentine flag and an officer's ceremonial sword. I knew that there was quite a collection of these items being held along with the enemy senior officers.

I said that if he would be so kind as to spirit an example of each to me discreetly, I could trade him unlimited quantities of gin. I had confiscated many bottles of a Dutch brand that a number of Argentine officers had had about them. The bottles fitted perfectly into my long Sterling sub-machine-gun ammunition pouches, so long as one did not take up the space with ammunition. I used to buy tonic and the Halliday family and I would drink to the downfall of the Galtieri régime in 'enemy gin'.

Rod Bell's face was a silent mask of total horror. 'What of Argentine honour?' he snapped at last before turning abruptly on his heel and sweeping back along the sea-front road.

I nearly got to the point of cupping my hands to my mouth to shout after him that, in view of things like the shooting of the helicopter crews in the sea, the murder of white flag negotiators at Goose Green, the way some of their officers abandoned their men and the grenade booby traps and human faeces recently found in broken-into homes and the school, it did not impress me much.

However, it suddenly came to me that, at the lowest and poorest level, the deceived Argentine conscripts had done their best for a wrong cause. Many had died at their posts. I stayed silent and carried on as usual with the POWs. I never did get a flag and a sword for my Corps, neither did I ever see Rod Bell again.

As the quantity of POWs at last started to dwindle, I was able to spend more time in the delightful atmosphere of Leslie Halliday's house. It was almost impossible to believe that Leslie had been a British soldier in the Second World War; he looked about twenty years too young. He had served in the local Regiment, the Falkland Islands Defence Force. His wife, Peggy, was a trained nurse and a riveting raconteur of the invasion and occupation. Her brother served on a Royal Navy ship during the Falklands War.

It is often overlooked that, because the Falkland Islanders are British, they serve in Her Majesty's Forces just like the citizens of any other British region. Their male population provides a slightly higher percentage than average. A considerable number of Falkland Islanders were directly involved as servicemen in the saving of their land, families and community.

Longevity must be a by-product of the fresh-air lifestyle, as I was introduced to Leslie's parents, who seemed totally well, though they must have been of a great age. Peggy's father, Archie, lived with his daughter and son-in-law. When life finally became almost normal again, he kept me company on local liaison strolls around the Port Stanley pubs.

Because of their sociability, hospitality and enjoyable company, the large Halliday kitchen had a constant stream of daytime tea and cake and evening cocktail guests. There were representatives from every area of the Task Force and the island community. Life in the place was a constant pageant of fine and noble people with fascinating tales to tell of recent events.

A teenage soldier of 2 Para stays very significantly in my memory. He might have been loud and crudely bragging like new young soldiers often are, but he was not. He was mature, rational, and listened to, and was considerate of, others. I had seen it before a number of times but it will never cease to impress or sadden me. The sudden spectacle of the fact that 'in the midst of life we are in death' had advanced him by many years. He was perhaps a more likeable young man as he now was, but he should not have had to learn like that. He should have been permitted a bit more of his lighthearted and careless youth. During the closing stages of the Darwin/Goose Green battle, the boy had been tasked to guard and give company to his dying Commanding Officer.

The Royal Navy was very proud, after the war, of its only prize ship, renamed the *Black Pig*, yet I do not think that they have ever acknowledged the man who gave it to them. On 15 June, 1982, Leslie

Halliday, in his Royal Navy-style uniform, saw that a small Argentine vessel was still flying its national flag after the surrender had been signed. He therefore requested an armed Royal Marine to accompany him and he strode on board and ordered the Argentine Captain to strike his colours. Leslie then gave the flag to his Royal Marine escort for his unit, and reported to the Royal Navy that he had just increased the Fleet.

Before I left the war, and again on my post-war visit, I sent letters to areas of authority – Royal Navy and my own Service – who, I felt, should be concerned. However, I am not aware that anything has been done. One can, of course, encounter resentment from a few who miss out on wars, but I am sorry that nothing did ever percolate through to someone who might have taken some action.

One afternoon on one of the last days of June, 1982, I was sitting in the general office at Government House and looking through some more Argentine documents that I had found, even at this late stage, when the full-Colonel Chief of Staff strode in.

'A useless mouth!' he said pointing at me. He then fell about laughing at my obvious mortification.

'No,' he continued, shaking his head kindly. 'I have just got to try and prune us down all I can. 3 Brigade may have set off home on *Canberra* yesterday but there are still too many of us now that it's all over and the Argies are gone. We are running out of food!' And he looked at me with his eyebrows raised in concern.

'I was keeping you to talk with the Antarctic islands POWs, who arrive today, but London says that they just want them sent straight home. 5 Brigade from over at Fitzroy and some appointments are going to stay for a while to help with the clear-up and normalization. However, I am afraid that I don't really think that your job has any post-war use!'

He went on to state that the first British Hercules aircraft since the war was going to attempt to get in during the next few hours. There was a blizzard raging outside.

The seating priority in order was: key people needed for high-level post-war discussions in London, compassionate case servicemen (family tragedies during the war), special forces personnel (they had had a far longer war than anyone else) and, finally, odds and ends like myself who were no longer required.

I was told by a more junior member of the Staff that my chances of getting a seat were not good. However, they would get me on to another aircraft or a ship as soon as they could.

I was sorry at the thought of leaving the Hallidays at such short notice. However, ships daily disgorged ever more high-ranking bores in gleaming combat suits. The word 'normalization' was being unceasingly used and I could see that Standing Orders and other such necessities for peacetime military communities were imminent. Many of us had been temporarily spoiled by the wartime luxury of greater licence to decide personally what action was required in a specific circumstance.

From some points of view, therefore, I was not sorry to leave at that moment. There was a feeling of 'ENDEX' among the combatants. What had been ordered had been done. It had been done with hardship, sacrifice, determination, innovation, occasional fear, revulsion and strong emotion, order, organization, physical alteration and agony for some – and luck.

I was not alone in feeling that it might be the moment to go home, before new times reduced a saga so dramatic that sometimes you could not believe that it had happened or that you could possibly have taken part in it to some sort of Falklands' pre-reorganization phase.

Leslie drove me, the military kit that I had not given to others who had to stay a while longer, and my Argentine items for my Museum and Corps' Messes to Port Stanley airfield.

I called that location 'the airfield' on my post-war tour and the Station Commander flew into a fury and said that I was to call it an 'operational RAF airbase', without either listening or comprehending that I was referring to times past.

The snowstorm or blizzard was gathering force and I doubted if even the imperturbable RAF transport pilots would attempt a landing, especially as it would be dark soon.

I bade Leslie goodbye. The dour Falklands folk do not go in for display, so I made sure that I made no embarrassing speech of farewell, but I was surprised at how much it hurt to contemplate leaving the islands and its people. My four previous campaigns had not really had a conclusion to give as a gift to those one fought for.

I said that I should try to get back to see Peggy, Archie and himself. I could not have realized that it would happen after eighteen months – and how totally different would be the circumstances.

The terminus building had lost some of its walls during one of the

Vulcan bomber raids. We prospective passengers huddled in the most protected corner of what remained of the waiting room. It was open to the sky in some areas. The front door, judging by the fragments scattered about, had once consisted of wire-reinforced frosted glass. However, it was now just a metal frame. One could have walked, unimpaired, straight through it, but chaps kept on opening it before going through the doorway, and then closing it again behind them.

If anyone forgot to shut it, there would be roars of 'Shut that bloody door!' and 'Were you born in a barn?'

The servicemen would dart back with a sheepish grin and a quick 'sorry' and would pull or push the handle to click the empty frame back onto its latch. I became fascinated by the sequence and it distracted me a bit from the unchanging sleet-laden gale that blew around us.

After a couple of hours a Staff Captain in the Cavalry walked in and announced, 'It'll be overhead in a minute.' He had been sitting in a jeep, monitoring the radio messages.

We all trudged, cold and soaked, out on to the concrete apron 'outside', and, unmistakeably, from somewhere high above the dark swirling sleet and snow, we heard the Hercules' engines.

'They'll never land,' the Staff Officer said and there was certainly no one who disagreed with him.

However, the sound came lower, and then, unbelievably, a great cylindrical belly and some huge wheels came racing towards us along the almost ground-level visibility ceiling.

Perhaps that landing was not an unusual achievement for a Hercules pilot, but we ground soldiers could not stop gaping and exclaiming. Absolutely nothing could be seen, a furious gale swirled across the airfield and, apart from having roughly filled bomb craters along it, the runway was a skid pan of slush. It was another breathtaking performance of an already larger-than-life two months.

It was obvious that there were too many of us, even for that giant container, so I was not surprised when the Cavalry Officer told my tail end of the queue, with a quick apology, that we would not get on.

Staff Clerks loaded their mail bags on to their truck, stores were stacked beside the runway and some, probably Ministry of Defence, senior Staff Officers got off. I hoped that, whatever their messages were, they would not disturb the General whom we worshipped.

I studied the aircraft and the busy crew for a while before I slung my kitbag onto my shoulder and, holding my lightened pack like a suitcase, stepped off to start the wet two miles back to Stanley.

'Pssst!' It was the sort of call made by a naughty postcard seller from the corner of an alley. I looked round and, just under the slope of the great tail, was an RAF Loadmaster. He glanced around him and then beckoned to me. I walked over and, steering me round to the lee of his aircraft, he said, 'Look, the Captain says that he can't promise anything. I mean, the doors are closed now. But if you hang about – don't make it too obvious – and if he's got any space or weight left, we'll get you on!'

'OK?' He finished, giving me a conspiratorial wink and a thump on the upper arm. With a movement of his eyes and head, he indicated that I should move quickly away from him. I was just stepping off when he called after me in a loud whisper, 'You'll have to run for it, all right? As he's taxiing . . . up over the tailgate. We've turned some fairly senior "pongos" down, so they would be pretty upset if they saw. Right?'

I silently smiled my thanks and gave a 'thumbs-up' that only he and I could see. I was perplexed as to why the aircrew should be so especially nice to me. Then it dawned – my beret. I had been an army soldier until two years earlier. Since transferring to the RAF Regiment I had spent much time training alongside the Army and I had been in units that were under Army command in both Northern Ireland and the Falklands War. It was, at times, too easy to forget who owned and paid me and that the thing that sat on my head was in RAF colours. It was loyalty, as well as friendship, that they gave me.

I studied Argentine wreckage along the side of the runway from the terminus, contemplated the indescribable weather and marvelled at the revving aircraft. Meanwhile, the others for whom, sadly, there was no space on this occasion, had already been given lifts back to town.

The pilot swivelled his colossal machine so that its still open rear was away from, and 'blind' to, the terminus; the Loadmaster made frantic gestures from the lowered 'drawbridge' and I tore after the already departing aircraft.

I hurled my kit on board and my friend and his colleague dragged me up and over the high ledge by the shoulder straps of my webbing. My furiously twinkling boots left the runway and I rolled inside. There was no seat for me, so I was strapped to a secured load.

Almost immediately after I got on the aircraft turned and the engines roared into take-off. The Hercules was pointed north. It was pointed towards my wife and children. It was pointed towards my parents, my brother, my friends and my home. I had not realized what it would feel like. I had not thought about it. I looked around at my comrades in that space and they too had been suddenly gripped. The journey back had started.

During the 9000-mile flight north, in those moments when I could take my mind off the excruciating discomfort of the plane's canvas seats, I mulled over in my mind the events of the past three months.

'A close-run thing' were apparently the words that the Iron Duke used after the Battle of Waterloo. I doubt that, once the first Royal Marine or Paratrooper had paddled ashore at San Carlos, the British would ever have been hurled back into the sea or decisively defeated on the Falklands. However, the phrase can be used in so far as it was a 'close-run thing' that victory was achieved in the time it was.

By the last battles around Port Stanley food and all kinds of ammunition were running out and Britain's finest infantrymen, although they had not faltered, were becoming worn down by the endless and worsening cold and damp of sub-Antarctic autumn and early winter. High steep slopes, hard rock, bog and tussock clumps make the Falklands one of the hardest terrains in the world for the human to cross on foot.

The sinking of the container ship *Atlantic Conveyor* meant that items like tents to dry out in and spare waterproof clothing were not available at the end of a terrible advance before a hard battle. Despite excellent pre-war instruction and disciplined prophylactic drills, trench foot was approaching epidemic levels. The poor design and paper-thin leather of the British military boot of the day, combined with ground that was like a water-filled sponge, even at the top of hills, gave men little chance ever to have dry feet.

The war could possibly have bogged down into a sort of First World War Western Front during the imminent harsh winter, while our commanders waited resupply and reinforcement. This would have given Britain's supporters and the UN time to start caving in and compromising, as always happens if things go on for too long, and the 'oppose-the-rescue-because-Margaret-Thatcher-and-her-Ministers-implemented-it' groups and the automatic, unenquiring and uncomprehending, simpleton 'peace' mobs, would have had time and excuse to grow. Rent-a-crowd rioters might have got themselves organized. Civilian resolve might have started to drain away, bleatings about the monetary cost of honour would have become a possibility and the Falkland Islanders' chances of being left as prisoners of a totally alien, fascist military could have increased.

They may still have problems one day. With the probable exception of Sir Anthony Eden, Margaret Thatcher has been the only British Prime Minister since Sir Winston Churchill to have had the strength and courage to 'nail her colours to the mast', heedless of personal career, on difficult points of principle.

About two years after the war, when work on the new Falklands airbase, RAF Mount Pleasant, had just started, a *Punch* cartoon showed the President of Argentina saying to an aide, 'If we don't push it too fast, we could get a decent runway.'

However, for the British nation and its Falklands Task Force, the 'close-run thing' was, within a matter of time, to be a far greater victory than could ever have been imagined.

On 17 June, 1982, General Galtieri and his fellow Junta members, who were responsible for the criminal act of putting Britons and Argentines in a situation where they had to kill each other over an incorrect and illegal 'cause', were thrown out of office and into prison. After another short, and more benign, military régime, civilian government re-established itself in Argentina. Thus we also 'liberated' the Argentinians!

Unknown to most outsiders, the Falkland Islanders had been kept like the landless serfs of earlier centuries by their commercial landlord, the Falkland Islands Company and its associate, 'Coalite'. The outside scrutiny brought about by the war uncovered this injustice and the Falklands farmers can now buy the sheep farms they work so hard.

The Falklands economy was in terminal decline as the world demand for wool lessened. The war drew attention to this and investment and the founding of other industries has since occurred. The first new houses, roads and public facilities built for decades have appeared.

All the world's great fishing nations used to send their fleets of hi-tech ocean vacuum-cleaner ships to the Falklands and South Georgia seas, which are the richest in the world. Now they must pay licence fees and the islands' Government has a very respectable income.

At the time I left East Falkland, in the first post-war British

Hercules and in a blinding snowstorm, the clean-up, repair and mine clearance of Port Stanley was well under way. Initially British soldiers had supervised work gangs of POWs. In addition to careless behaviour and shedding rubbish everywhere, the Argentines had a habit of defecating on living-room carpets, chairs, beds and in cupboards. They left hand-grenade booby traps under cups in kitchens, attached to civilian front gates and about the school.

According to the Geneva Convention, minefields must be mapped and recorded. Different commands of the Argentine military had, without co-ordination, scattered unrecorded mines. Many of them are a plastic type that defy metal detectors. There is still a steady attrition of Falklands livestock and a series of post-war Royal Engineer commanders, and a number of their men, have died trying to clear these mines by the only method possible – on their knees, prodding with a short spike.

'Splice the Mainbrace!' Her Majesty had ordered, I recalled as we flew north, when victory was confirmed. One could, of course, more easily comply with this order if one had a dwelling and a rum store. However, we on shore, and not in a Royal Navy warship, did our best, in our farm and dockside sheds and with confiscated enemy bottles or items bought from Stanley shops, to obey our Sovereign's command!

The lessons of the war, which in some cases were learned the hard way, were not to be lost. One was the determination of the heads of all British Armed Forces of the period. The event had been the first sudden conventional warlike adventure for nearly two generations, and it is no bad idea to avoid future 'close-run things' if possible!

In-depth interviews were conducted with every military unit that went to the war, even the most obscure, which, of course, included Her Majesty's Interrogators.

All three of us in my unit were separately interviewed and I was delighted to note that the first point made in the ensuing pamphlet was the need for a properly constituted Interrogation/POW Handling Unit to be deployed early in future conventional conflicts, as opposed to the way my team set off and got through it all.

My two SNCOs got awards or commendations for their sterling behind-the-scenes part in the war. Sadly, they were not at the level that I recommended. However, the appreciation must be different when viewed from chains-of-command who were not at the event.

Three Argentine Brigades had been repatriated with just the set of clothes that each man stood up in, and items belonging to the Argentine navy and air force had also been confiscated; so the British forces acquired a considerable amount of military equipment. Not all of it could be put to use by the British system.

The first British troops into Port Stanley tore bits off Iroquois helicopters, Pucara aircraft and Panhard armoured cars as souvenirs for barrack block walls and unit clubs, particularly squares of fuselage or parts with Argentine crests, flags or roundels on them. However, all the Argentine high-class military vehicles went to the Falkland Islands Defence Force. Unfortunately, the Argentines had not yet paid for them, so the German manufacturers started sending their final demands for payment to the British. Some sort of accord was eventually reached over this.

Oerlikon anti-aircraft guns and working military aircraft were returned to Britain, and some of the Argentine small arms were suitable for Britain's reservist forces. The smaller ex-Argentine aircraft and naval vessels remained on the Falklands as transporters and carriers between the islands.

After about five hours of the flight back home word was passed back from the pilots that the *Canberra* was below. Many of us had watched enviously as she had set sail from Port Stanley on 22 June, two days before our departure from the airfield.

From the aircraft's porthole-like windows we could just see *Canberra* directly below us and determinedly steaming in the same direction that we were flying. She looked pretty, but ghostly, with her many lights on the dark and misty sea.

We all smirked over the fact that we should arrive ahead of the thousands of Royal Marines on board. However, a week later, when she sailed into Southampton and a welcome from the British people that has gone down in history, I am sure that every one of my fellow aircraft passengers felt as I did. I would have given almost anything to have been with them.

Once again Ascension Island cheered and rejuvenated as its dry heat cleared the sub-Antarctic damp from every recess of the body. There was a Wing of my Corps guarding the island. They let me use their hot shower and canteen. I had a full cooked breakfast and, though the seemingly permanent tiredness remained, I actually felt something less than forty and could possibly have broken into a jog about the airfield pathways.

We arrived at RAF Lyneham at two in the morning and I was given a tiny room in a Nissen hut and the cosiest little iron bed since the world began. The following afternoon the cooks made me a wonderful meal, even though it was outside any meal time, and transport for Catterick arrived.

As always, when I beheld her after a period of parting, I had difficulty believing that the slender, elegant girl who greeted me was really mine. My wife had organized a little gathering of my friends for my evening homecoming.

My son hugged one of my legs hard, because that was all he could reach, and my little daughter allowed herself to be picked up and kissed. She immediately recounted her current pursuance to me. It was hitting all the small boys in the area.

Two days after arriving back at the RAF Regiment Depot a very Senior Officer from the part of the Royal Air Force hierarchy that ruled my Corps arrived on an inspection. His tour would, of course, include a visit to the Museum. I was on a week's leave. However, the visit was a privilege for the camp and so I was, of course, waiting in the foyer at the appropriate time to show him round.

The Senior Officer had a charming and academic manner and looked, as I believe is the case, as if he had risen up the staff, rather than the soldier, ladder. All went well until we got right to the end of the historical circuit and back by the entrance. He asked me why space had been made beyond the Northern Ireland section. I said that I had cleared it to make a Falklands War display and started enthusiastically to run through the trophies that I had been lucky enough to gain for it.

'What has the Falklands to do with the RAF Regiment?' he roared and swept out of the building so fast that he left his entourage of senior Staff Officers behind – for a few moments.

I stood alone, bewildered as to how I could have offended. A Depot Senior Officer returned as I was starting to lock up and put the lights out. He was one whom I had always thought of as a decent chap but a bit of a 'stuffed shirt'. I was wrong. He was kind, thoughtful and principled. He outlined to me a sad tale that I could not have known about, or imagined.

A Royal fortieth anniversary parade for the Corps had occurred while I was in the Falklands. Questions were apparently asked in high places as to why a 'fortieth anniversary'. Twenty-fifth or fiftieth are the normal milestones that merit the attention of Her Majesty. The Senior Officer that I had offended was the inspiration and motivation behind it, and he had eventually prevailed.

The war had been cruelly untimely and had risked taking a number of Corps Units and preventing the turnout of a 'full set'. An impressive number of men, obviously, had to be on parade. Effort was apparently made to ensure that Army units, of similar skills to those of the RAF Regiment, filled all the gaps caused by the war and the historic ceremony not be prejudiced. However, a Wing, a Rapier Squadron and a number of individuals, including myself, had been lost. The war had also, of course, distracted a lot of attention on the actual day of the parade, which was understandably distressing for those who had put such a lot of effort into it.

It had been thought that the Senior Officer might have got a knighthood. However, possibly because the melodramatic events in the South Atlantic were overshadowing so much at the time, it had not eventuated. However, he did receive a high peacetime decoration and his new photograph was already in the entrance halls of the Corps' Messes and headquarters.

My inadvertently discourteous behaviour had sadly not ended with that afternoon. For the Senior Officers' dinner that was held in the Mess that night, the Mess Steward, probably to give a topical note, had placed a bronze equestrian statuette, that I had provided, of General José de San Martin, the South American rebel victor over Imperial Spain, as the centrepiece to the cocktail snacks table.

'Get that thing out of my sight,' the Senior Officer said as he entered the room. 'I do not wish to be constantly reminded that one of my officers is a thief!'

General José spent the evening in the ladies' lavatory.

I also heard that I featured throughout the meal. I could not have imagined that I should have queried my order to go to war. Probably, if I had, a very high level would have had it rescinded.

As is usual when an officer errs on a matter of significant principle, Staff Officers are directed to make notes on the spot and ensure that the offender never prospers.

Some middle-ranking officers of the RAF Regiment resigned because they were unhappy with the Corps during the Falklands war period. At some military levels, and not always where it should be, there can be too much honour.

Attitudes, even in the supposedly ultra-conservative British armed forces, are changing. I entered an RAF Officers' Mess one evening on my post-war tour to East Falkland just in time to hear a Senior Officer say that, during the war, a pilot from his command or unit had told his superior that he did not think that he could cope with his posting to the war.

The officer continued, 'Well you have to admire him. He had the courage to step forward and speak out.'

'His OC should have shot him,' I said, mostly out of curiosity to see how they would react. There was no anger. They just thought that I was comical.

Film-makers have also been disappointing about the war. There were so many stirring tales and 'ripping yarns'; yet, as far as I am aware, the only full-length feature film made was the story of the Scots Guardsman who was lost, or wandered, during the Battle of Tumbledown.

There has been a television film that portrayed a wounded officer discontented with his post-war treatment and his ex-service Medical Officer father who 'pulled rank' on officers still serving. However, there has been a very realistic television reconstruction of Governor Hunt's brave, but doomed, stand at the start of it all. If military men do well, they unnerve and anger the manhood of some members of the more egotistical professions.

When the fighting was over I listened to a group of soldiers joking about how Hollywood might present the saga. The hero, they decided, would have to be an American Vietnam veteran who was now a scientist studying something unique to the Falklands. He would have a Starlet as a Falklands Island girlfriend. When war occurs, he will be an unrelievedly heroic marksman with a hip-fired machine gun that has an endless magazine and never gets stoppages. He will sort out the waffling and Blimpish British officers and their well-intentioned but thick troops and lead them to victory. However, in order not to upset United States/Latin America relations, all 'enemy' who are jerked backwards with exploding sachets of tomato ketchup under the front of their combat jackets will be from a 'rogue' or 'bandit' breakaway unit of unimaginable evil. This will justify their treatment.

Amateur mercenaries were summarily shot by us, some Guardsmen were captured and tortured to death. Rumours, many and various, have circulated since the war. Some even gave rise to a British war crimes investigation. I, of course, heard many of the rumours. However, I doubt almost all of them. The war was a sudden and dramatic event, and the first full-scale war that almost all participants had attended. When men met up with other groups, there was a tendency to try and astound them with a good 'tale' and have the fun of knowing that in those 'anything-could-happen' times one would very likely be believed.

In the last forlorn days as the West's politically sabotaged stand in Indo-China was collapsing, so many of my companions serving with local allied forces were killed that I think I left that war ashamed to be alive. This only occurred to me when the Falklands War ended.

I did not wish my life to end, of course; I just felt that I had failed by not doing what others had done and got killed. The Falklands caused a feeling, that I did not put into clear thought at the time, that I was being given a second chance.

A gate that I had once not managed to pass through was waiting for me again. Though in a different place, it was the same gate. A bus that I had missed twelve years before had stopped too far down the road for me to run after it. Presumably my dead friends would be sitting on it!

My 'cure' was that 'the gate' obviously did not want me that time either! I loved my calling and, of course, my family. However, something in the intervening years ensured that I was always somewhat detrimentally distracted.

For whatever reason, the Falklands War has lightened thoughts, feelings and memories, subconscious or whatever, of another earlier event. Maybe the Falklands War finally ended the Vietnam War for me!

In seven weeks a task force of 28,000 men and over 100 ships was assembled. It sailed 8,000 miles and fought off combat aircraft that outnumbered its own by six to one. 10,000 men were landed on a hostile coast. The men on land prevailed in about a dozen pitched battles and skirmishes against an enemy in fortified defensive positions who invariably outnumbered them. The enemy were brought to surrender within three and a half weeks.

Nearly 300 Britons and three times that number of Argentines lost their lives. The wounded, many horribly maimed and permanently disabled, are three times these numbers.

I estimate the average age of our servicemen in the war to have been in their early twenties. Ninety percent of the officers and men had never before been under fire. The British nation cannot have had better servants.

Among so many scenes and sensations that pass and repass through my heart and memory, there is an encounter from the moment the fighting finished that provokes a thought or two. As I approached Port Stanley across the dramatic battlefields of the Argentines' last stands, I passed by a teenage Paratrooper, now in his maroon beret. He was on his own and he jerked his head this way and that as he still tried to take in the scenes about him. Weapons and scattered kit were being gathered into piles, dead were being buried and near us was a pit with a headless corpse in it where a Milan missile, probably, had hit an Argentine heavy machine-gun bunker.

'When you join the Army,' he said, not caring who I was but needing someone to tell his feelings to, 'I mean you expect maybe to go to somewhere like Northern Ireland, don't you?' He stared fixedly into my face. 'But you don't expect anything like this!'

I gave him what I hoped was a companionable and understanding smile and trudged on towards the racecourse and the coast road. On the face of it, what he said was totally illogical. What else should a soldier expect but that? However, what had just happened to him had happened to me a few years before, so I knew what he meant and I knew how he felt.

Index

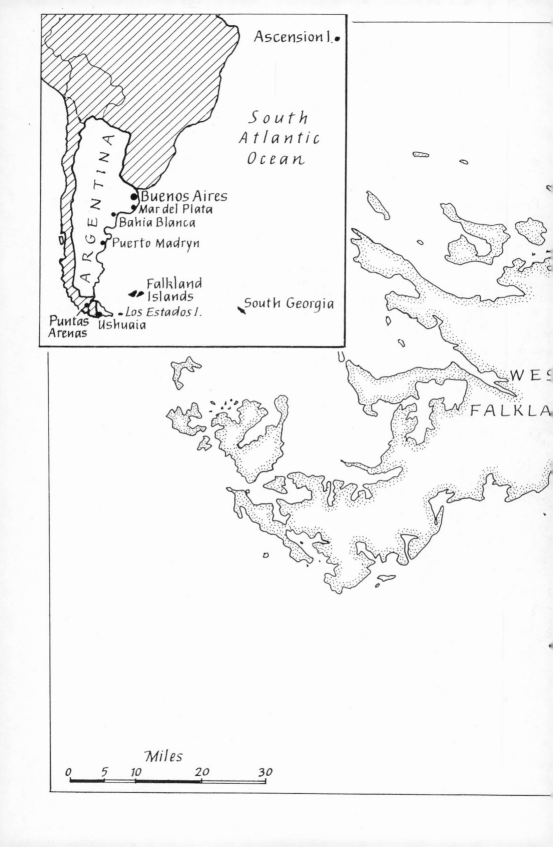

Ascension I.

South
Atlantic
Ocean

ARGENTINA

Buenos Aires
Mar del Plata
Bahia Blanca
Puerto Madryn

Falkland
Islands

South Georgia

Los Estados I.

Puntas
Arenas   Ushuaia

WES

FALKLA

Miles

0   5   10   20   30